DEDICATION

My first joy in life is being a wife and mother with all it encompasses. My second joy in life is being a professional writer and author. I am one of the lucky few that get to have it all.

Therefore, this book is dedicated to my dear and loving husband, Keith, who believes in me completely. It is also dedicated to my children, Matthew, Kimberly, Rebekah, and Katherine, who are so incredibly supportive of my work. Without my family's blessings, this book would still be an unwritten manuscript.

Thank you for loving me and trusting in my abilities.

We recently lost our beloved pet "Bear," who was not only our best and dearest friend but also the "Vice President of Sunshine" here at Atlantic Publishing. He did not receive a salary but worked tirelessly 24 hours a day to please his parents. Bear was a rescue dog that turned around and showered myself, my wife Sherri, his grandparents Jean, Bob and Nancy and every person and animal he met (maybe not rabbits) with friendship and love. He made a lot of people smile every day.

We wanted you to know that a portion of the profits of this book will be donated to The Humane Society of the United States.

–Douglas & Sherri Brown

The Complete Guide to

Your First Rental Property

A Step-by-Step Plan from the

Experts Who Do It Every Day

By Teri B. Clark

The Complete Guide to Your First Rental Property: A Step-by-Step Plan from the Experts Who Do It Every Day

ISBN-13: 978-0-910627-98-6   ISBN-10: 0-910627-98-3

Library of Congress Cataloging-in-Publication Data

Clark, Teri B.
  The complete guide to your first rental property : a step-by-step plan
from the experts who do it every day / by Teri B. Clark.
      p. cm.
  Includes bibliographical references and index.
  ISBN-13: 978-0-910627-98-6
  ISBN-10: 0-910627-98-3
  1. Rental housing--United States--Management. 2. Real estate
investment--United States. 3. Real estate management--United States.
  I. Title.
  HD1394.5.U6C63 2008
  643'.2--dc22
                    2007049095

INTERIOR LAYOUT DESIGN: Vickie Taylor • vtaylor@atlantic-pub.com

Printed on Recycled Paper

Printed in the United States

THE HUMANE SOCIETY
OF THE UNITED STATES ©

The human-animal bond is as old as human history. We cherish our animal companions for their unconditional affection and acceptance. We feel a thrill when we glimpse wild creatures in their natural habitat or in our own backyard.

Unfortunately, the human-animal bond has at times been weakened. Humans have exploited some animal species to the point of extinction.

The Humane Society of the United States makes a difference in the lives of animals here at home and worldwide. The HSUS is dedicated to creating a world where our relationship with animals is guided by compassion. We seek a truly humane society in which animals are respected for their intrinsic value, and where the human-animal bond is strong.

Want to help animals? We have plenty of suggestions. Adopt a pet from a local shelter, join The Humane Society and be a part of our work to help companion animals and wildlife. You will be funding our educational, legislative, investigative and outreach projects in the U.S. and across the globe.

Or perhaps you'd like to make a memorial donation in honor of a pet, friend or relative? You can through our Kindred Spirits program. And if you'd like to contribute in a more structured way, our Planned Giving Office has suggestions about estate planning, annuities, and even gifts of stock that avoid capital gains taxes.

Maybe you have land that you would like to preserve as a lasting habitat for wildlife. Our Wildlife Land Trust can help you. Perhaps the land you want to share is a backyard—that's enough. Our Urban Wildlife Sanctuary Program will show you how to create a habitat for your wild neighbors.

So you see, it's easy to help animals. And The HSUS is here to help.

The Humane Society of the United States
2100 L Street NW
Washington, DC 20037
202-452-1100
www.hsus.org

TABLE OF CONTENTS

FOREWORD

Karen Ebert, REALTOR®, MPM®, RMP®, e-PRO
President, Austin Landmark Property Services, Inc. ALPS

"This was one of the best investments I've ever made." This statement was sweet music to our ears from one of our clients. The investor had done his homework before leaping into the realm of residential real estate investment. He had spent many years studying the field and all the complex factors that would impact his investment success or failure. As a result, he had reached his financial goals through his investment portfolio.

More often, we hear the opposite comment as clients jump into the unknown waters of real estate investment with little or no preparation or guidance.

As a professional property management company for over 20 years, we have come to believe that the majority of our clients would have had less stressful and more financially successful experiences with owning investment properties had they prepared in advance of making their decisions.

The valuable resources in Teri B. Clark's book First Rental Property would have enabled our clients to evaluate and choose better investment properties, decide whether to manage their properties or hire a professional property manager, and establish an efficient plan for building their portfolio.

Real estate agents and realtors have expertise in serving the needs of an owner occupant buyer or seller. However, when it comes to meeting the needs of a new residential real estate investor they sometimes lack the education and experience to guide the client through the process of real estate investment. *The Complete Guide to Your First Rental Property* can be an educational tool for the agent as they endeavor to give the best possible service to their clients and make residential real estate investment their niche.

Included in *The Complete Guide to Your First Rental Property* are informative case studies by expert professionals in the industry. These case studies give prospective investors a realistic view of being a landlord. In the case studies, contributors to the book highlight the challenges landlords face and explore the potential solutions to those challenges.

The Complete Guide to Your First Rental Property's Appendix is a stand alone asset. This section gives investors resources, checklists, guidelines, sample forms and examples that can help decrease the learning curve. The forms and tables in the appendix can help investors avoid pitfalls that could undermine their goals.

Occasionally, we have the opportunity to consult with an investor prior to their first purchase of investment property. Now we feel fortunate to have such a great resource in Teri B. Clark's informative book. Now we better assist our clients in getting off to the best start as a first time investor in real estate.

Karen earned her Broker license in 1983 and has specialized in property management since that time, In addition to being a REALTOR®, she is a founding member of the National Association of Residential Property Managers and served as Vice-president of NARPM® from October 1988 through September 1992. She holds the RMP® (Residential Management Professional) and MPM® (Master Property Manager) designations of the association. Karen also holds the e-PRO designation from the National Association of Realtors indicating her level of Internet expertise. As editor of the NARPM® newsletter, Karen has had the opportunity to keep abreast of the very latest in the profession. She had contributed to the association by writing and presenting three workshops for the annual convention, Karen was instrumental in starting the Austin Area Chapter of NARPM® where she served as the first President and has been awarded Member of the Year for her efforts in producing the chapter newsletter.

Karen oversees the operational functions of ALPS, Inc., which has earned the Certified Residential Management Company designation from the National Association of Residential Property Managers. Her goals in property management are to provide efficient and honest handling of owner and resident funds, timely reporting, thorough documentation of files and on-going staff training to assure the highest level of caring service to clients and residents.

INTRODUCTION

If you want to build wealth, real estate is one way to do it, and investing in rental property is one of the most popular real estate options today. This is due to potential rewards as the property appreciates in value, while tenants pay the expenses of the investment.

Of course, any investment has its drawbacks. Managing tenants is a drawback to investing in rental property. Such management includes finding tenants, keeping them, and sometimes evicting them. There are also rules and regulations, state and federal laws, maintenance issues, and rent collections to deal with.

Time is another issue to consider. Rental properties do not create instant wealth. They are a long term investment with profits coming from appreciation of the property in the market. The money does not come in the actual rental of the property, but in the value of the real estate over time.

Investing in rental property is not something to enter into lightly. This type of investment involves far more than collecting the rent check each month.

To be a successful rental property investor, you do need to understand which properties will appreciate due to location, and you will need to collect those checks; but these things are only one component of success.

Beyond knowledge of the process, you need the mind-set it takes to be a real estate investor and landlord. Do you have what it takes to be a landlord? Do you have the time and energy required? Do you have the long-term vision that can get you through lean times?

Rental property investing takes work. You have to be involved in the process or employ people who are. This type of investing is not like buying a bond and then sitting back and waiting 10 years. You will have to be fully committed to owning property as a business venture.

By reading this book, you will acquire the skills you need to:

- Understand the investment aspects of rental properties compared to other investment opportunities.

- Understand the basics of being a landlord.

- Find available rental homes and choose the right one for you by determining whether the property will make money.

- Finance your investment property.

- Prepare your property for rent.

- Find good tenants.

- Manage tenant/landlord issues such as late fees, security deposits, and rental policies.

- Determine the repairs that need to be made and the services that need to be offered.

- Take advantage of the tax rules and avoid tax mistakes.

- Offer a lease option.

- Use the computer for your rental property investing.

- Retire using your investment funds as income.

You will also have access to the landlord tenant laws for all 50 states, documents for closing, word document templates, samples of leases and rental agreements, popular lease clauses, and home maintenance lists.

By the time you finish this book, you will have the knowledge you need to begin investing as a rental property owner. You will also understand what it takes to be a landlord, and you will have the skills and resources necessary to make this form of investing work for you.

INVEST IN THE BEST

THINK LONG-TERM

Each year, some investments are top performers while others fall short. Real estate falls into the latter category, but far less often than other investments. Real estate, when not inflated artificially, continues to appreciate.

Unlike many investments, real estate is tangible. It is not a piece of paper stating that you own shares, a bond showing that you have given a loan to the government, or a savings account with a receipt showing your money is there. Even money is just paper that states a value set by the government, backed in some form by gold reserves.

Real estate, on the other hand, is something you can see. You are in complete control when it comes to the improvement of your investment, and you determine when your investment property needs to have repairs or additions.

For some, control may not be good. If you prefer ease over control, then rental property investing is not for you.

THE PAST AND THE FUTURE

Real estate is one of the few investments that offers a secure and steady return on investment (ROI) even in times of uncertainty. Currently (2007), the United States is experiencing a dip. There are factors, however, that demonstrate the good outlook of real estate despite this dip.

The biggest factor is population. The population of the United States will continue to grow well into the future.

- By 2010, more than 40 percent of all households will be age 55 or older.

- In the next 30 years, people over the age of 65 will double to 70 million.

- In the next 20 years, 29 percent of all households will consist of only one person.

- By 2030, 60 percent of the population will live in a city.

- In the next 20 years, the Latino population will double.

With growth comes people getting married, having babies, and finding new jobs. Growth generates the need for new housing. Looking at these statistics, you may determine what kind of housing is best for your investments.

Understanding the demographics might lead you to purchase single-story homes to accommodate those over 55, or smaller homes to attract the single person household. You may decide that purchasing in the city is a good idea. Of course, each of these statistics will need to be gauged against the specific geographic area in which you intend to invest.

These demographics can also help you choose geographic locations. For instance, the Latino population will migrate mostly from Mexico, so border states will be growing. Looking at the aging population, you can assume that the Sunbelt states will grow as people in the northern states retire to a warmer climate.

Due to the ever-increasing population, the downward trend of real estate will eventually go up.

Investor Insight: Investing in real estate is always a good idea, as long as you are doing so long term. Investing in rental properties is good, even in times of a downward trend, because even those who cannot afford to buy will need a place to live, and renting a home is a good option.

RETIRE WITH PROPERTY

Building a retirement nest egg is one reason that people buy real estate. It is now possible to buy real estate using the retirement funds in your IRA or 401(k). To do so, you have to put your funds into a self-directed IRA or roll them over. A self-directed IRA allows you to make the financial decisions instead of leaving them to someone else, like a manager of a mutual fund.

Real estate held this way needs to be for the long term. You will get the benefits of the appreciation of your assets, but you will not be able to live off rental income until you have reached the age of 65½ without taking penalty losses. You will also be unable to deduct depreciation since the investment is not taxable. The increase in principle, however, is often enough to offset the negative aspects of holding real estate in an IRA.

It is imperative to know the rules regarding holding real estate in an IRA. Not knowing them can be devastating to you in fines and in taxes.

For instance, you are allowed to purchase any kind of property you would like with an IRA fund as long as you do not use that property for yourself. You may purchase a beach home as an investment property, but you may not use it for at least two weeks out of each year. After you retire, you can take the house out of your IRA as a distribution. Then, you can use the house any way you would like, but while it is in the IRA, you may not use it personally.

There is also the matter of who you may rent the property to. You cannot rent to your spouse or your direct ascendants or descendants, such as grandparents or children, but you can rent to your siblings, aunts, uncles, and cousins.

Investor Insight: There are many other rules relating to IRA real estate holdings. It is best to contact a lawyer well-versed in IRA real estate tax laws.

CASE STUDY: CHRIS LENGQUIST

Chris Lengquist, a real estate investor in the Kansas City area, believes that real estate is always a good investment. When asked why, he gives the following reasons:

- It is easily accessible to a wide variety of investors of all ages.
- Real estate can be leveraged.
- People know their neighborhood and the housing in their area and can capitalize on this knowledge.
- Over the long-haul, you cannot lose money with real estate.
- You get cash flow before taxes.

For Chris, it is also rewarding. "I take a certain amount of pride knowing that not only am I securing a retirement for me and my wife, but I am providing clean, safe, affordable housing to those not able or willing to purchase their own home."

But what about real estate market slumps? Should people avoid buying properties during times like these? Not according to Chris. "What difference does the market make? I buy when I have the money to get another house."

Chris believes that buying a home during a downturn is ideal. In his experience, it is easier to find better deals:

"There simply is no 'wrong time' to buy. If the property meets your credentials, then buy it. If you never buy because it is always the wrong time, you will end up with nothing in the end. Act now!"

CASE STUDY: CHRIS LENGQUIST

Although he currently only owns two properties, his goal is 10 to 14. Having this number of properties will meet the financial goals he has set. "I invest for growth, not cash flow. Any cash flow I get goes right back into the operating account. My pay-off is down the road." How many rentals you own, either more or less, will completely depend on your financial goals and abilities as an investor.

"To me, a good mix is three to four multi-family homes to every six or seven single-family homes. I have no problem with one in Kansas City, one in Tulsa, and one in Baton Rouge, as long as the home will pay for itself and its property manager."

According to Chris, knowing whether a property is a good rental property is simple. Simply ask yourself, "Will it make money?" You can determine whether a property will make money.

First, you have to know what ROI goals you are shooting for. You need to look at cash flow, principal reduction, depreciation, and appreciation. Then you can determine whether the property will give you those returns.

Be diligent in your pursuit of properties to find those that fit your criteria, such as location, type of property, or number of bedrooms. In addition to finding a property with the right criteria, you will need to see whether the goals you wish to reach can be reached in a timely manner. You will also need to look at the cash you have on hand. A professional real estate agent and/or counselor can help you here.

Chris says, "On your first deal or two, do not try to do it alone. Have someone with experience walk you through, and do not pick any old agent. Find one that knows real estate investing."

When a property fits, you need to finance it. "Leveraging your money means using other people's money. Whether it is a bank, a mortgage broker, or a private lender, you sell them on the investment and your real estate capabilities and you use their money for the bulk of the transaction."

Finding tenants can be difficult. Chris says, "I think I scare off quite a few prospective tenants, but I would rather be empty another month than get a bad tenant."

Here is his strategy:

- Make polite conversation peppered with questions that let you know who they are, where they work, and why they are moving.

- Tell them that you keep your units in good condition and expect them to do the same.

- Tell them that you will be in every 60 to 90 days to verify that the property does not have any new water leaks or other problems.

CASE STUDY: CHRIS LENGQUIST

- Inform them that you are an observant landlord and will be involved in the property.

These techniques may make some tenants disappear, but Chris has found that he is quite happy with those who are willing to stick around.

Chris is involved in the maintenance and upkeep of his properties. "I expect much from my tenants and I tell them so. So in return I turn a unit over to them that is clean, safe, freshly painted, and has clean carpeting. I do not rent a house with known defects. If they find one, they can call me right away and I will fix it. However, they know that if they did it, they fix it."

He watches the properties closely and goes through each property at least once every 90 days, even if it is just to replace a furnace filter.

"This gives me a chance to see how the property is being cared for. If I do not like something I see, I can take care of it then and there. I do not want to walk into a property after 12 to 24 months and find out the dog has been urinating on the carpet, the kids have been carving into the walls, and that the pipe under the bathroom sink has a slow leak."

Although Chris uses a lease drawn up by his attorney, he has this to say concerning leases: "I am a believer that if a tenant gets the urge to jump, they will. A lease is not going to do much good, unless I want to spend my time and my money tracking them down to sue them."

What has been Chris's best experience in the world of rental investments? "Any time a house does not hold a nasty surprise, it is a best experience. Do your homework, get inspections, and check the numbers two and three times. Do all that and you will find most experiences to be pleasant."

Chris Lengquist, RIPS
Keller Williams Realty
Diamond Partners, Inc.
www.listwithchris.net
listwithchris@kw.com
Phone: 913-322-7515
Fax: 913-322-8259

MORE THAN ONE WAY TO INVEST

Real estate investing can take many forms. Here are some of the options.

Speculation

When you invest in spec homes, you are buying a home with the expectation that the home will rise in value. To get the most appreciation, the investor buys low and sells high. Straightforward speculation investing means buying homes off the market or homes that are in the process of being built. These homes have no particular problems or issues, but you feel that the sale price is low and that you have the opportunity to sell at a higher price.

One advantage to investing in the speculation market is quick profit realization. If you time it right, you can make a good deal of money in just one year, especially if you were able to finance with a low down payment and you have many properties. This method of investing is common when times are good.

The difficulty with this form of real estate investing is determining when the time is right. The market can change suddenly, and if you have many properties that are not appreciating quickly enough, you can find yourself with expenses far exceeding any profits you could make.

Investor Insight: With speculation investing, you can plan to lose money each month. The key is that you believe, or speculate, that you will make that money back and more when you sell.

There are some ways to make this form of investing less risky. Look for job creation in the area. As jobs are created, housing demands increase. If, however, the job boom is not evident in your area, a national housing boom will not affect you, and you are likely to lose money.

You can also watch interest rates. Falling rates mean that homes are more affordable, giving you a better chance of someone being able to buy your home.

Finally, look at the boom of local fast food chains. Before restaurants such as McDonald's come into an area, market demographics are scrutinized. If there is not sufficient population or expected growth, new restaurants will not come to the area.

Speculation is a risky way to invest in real estate. If you do not have the money to lose each month until you can sell or have the money to hang on during the downward trends, then speculation is not a wise investment option for you.

Investing in Seized Property

Investing in seized property is similar to speculation. The main difference is that with seized property you have a far better chance of buying at a low price. Homes are seized when taxes are owed and have not been paid. The property is then sold off for the taxes, fines, and interest, or it is sold at auction.

Before purchasing a seized property, you need to find out:

- Whether the property is worth more than the taxes owed

- How the property is zoned

- What the state and local laws are concerning the rights of the previous owner

Like speculation properties, your hope is that you will buy low and sell high. The same pitfalls of speculation properties are attached to investing in seized property.

Fixer-Uppers

A fixer-upper home is one that needs a number of repairs and renovations to be of similar value to the homes around it. If you invest in a fixer-upper, you intend to buy the distressed house at a low price, fix it up, and then sell it at a premium price.

Fixer-uppers are another kind of speculative venture. Taking a distressed home and making it live up to the standards of the neighborhood can be costly. It also involves making the assumption that you are going to be able to bring the house up to the standard required.

One way to lessen the risk of the speculative nature of this kind of investing is to have more than one fixer-upper property. This way, if one property loses money, you have another to make up that loss.

The heavy taxes on gains are another disadvantage. Each time you sell a home, you have to pay a capital gains tax. Since the home will not be your primary residence, the entire tax will be due even if you use the profits to buy a home of higher value.

Live In It and Then Sell It

One way to invest in real estate is to buy a home, live in it while you are fixing it up, and then sell it. As long as you live in the home for at least two years, it will be considered your primary residence and capital gains will be eliminated.

Since you plan to live on-site, you are more likely to have done your homework concerning the location. Once again, you need to buy low. The best way to buy low is to look for a home that does not quite meet the standards of the surrounding neighborhood.

A home may be just below the standards of the surrounding neighborhood due to:

- Low-end kitchen
- Inadequate number of bathrooms

- Small closets
- Lack of landscaping
- Out-of-date woodwork, wallpaper, color scheme, or appliances

If you are willing to live in a house undergoing renovations, this strategy may be a good way to invest. The biggest risk involved is that you end up putting more money into the home than you can get out of it. The major benefit of this kind of investment is that while you are selling, you are living in the home, which means that you are deriving a benefit while the home is on the market.

Private Mortgage Investing

A private mortgage happens when you loan private money to an individual buying a home, and this borrower cannot meet the requirements for a conventional loan. These loans are short-term (six months to three years) loans and they are based on the value of the property instead of the borrower's credit.

The advantages to private mortgage investing are many:

- High interest rate on your investment

- Monthly income

- Secure investment — as long as you have done your homework on the true value of the home

Before investing in a mortgage, you need to understand the loan-to-value ratio, which is not as technical as it sounds. It is the ratio of the loan on the mortgage compared to the value of the mortgage, and it is found by dividing the loan by the mortgage value.

For example, if you loan $70,000 on a $100,000 house, your loan-to-value (LTV) is 70 percent. If you only loaned $50,000, then your LTV would be

50 percent. The lower your LTV, the safer your investment. Most successful private mortgage investors do not loan out more than a 70 percent LTV.

Whenever you decide to lend money privately on a mortgage, it is imperative that you check out the property yourself. The home may be located in an area that has a good reputation, but that should not be enough for you. The house may be rundown or it may be far smaller than you were led to believe. The house may also be poorly located within a good neighborhood — i.e., next to the community dump or loud park.

Investor Insight: You are lending money and your money will be safe if your loan-to-value ratio is not more than 70 percent. The only way you can know this for sure is to see the home yourself.

Although private mortgage investing is a good way to invest, there are some associated cons. As with other real estate investing, it is not a liquid investment because you will have agreed to lend the money for a specified time. Additionally, you have to have at least $10,000 to invest to get started, and higher amounts will provide you with far more choices.

Real Estate Stocks

Another way to invest in real estate is through a Real Estate Investment Trust (REIT). A REIT is a fund that invests in stocks and bonds related to real estate.

Although you can invest in REIT companies privately, most people do so through a special mutual fund. The most popular way for these funds to be invested is by buying property (equity REIT). However, some REITs are set up to invest in mortgages (mortgage REIT) or a combination of property and mortgages (hybrid REIT).

You can invest in an equity REIT that focuses on only one type of property or on a variety of properties. Some possible property investments include:

- Apartments
- Medical buildings
- Offices
- Public self-storage
- Shopping centers
- Restaurants

- Hotels
- Warehouses
- Mobile home parks
- Regional malls
- Factory outlets
- Golf courses

With a REIT, you can build a diverse portfolio quickly. You can also get started with little investment.

There are, of course, drawbacks to investing in a REIT. A REIT can underperform in relation to the stock market. Additionally, the tax rate on a REIT does not qualify for the lower federal rate on dividends.

RENTAL DIVERSITY

There is more than one type of rental property to invest in:

- Rental homes
- Low income rentals
- Commercial real estate

- Rent-to-own homes
- Boarding homes

All these options have differing pros and cons. For instance, a rental home is a reliable long-term investment. The same holds true with low income housing, but you may find that you have more repair and tenant issues. With boarding homes, you will have the headache of large turnovers since those who rent only a room are often more transient than those who rent a home. Finally, when renting commercial real estate, you have to worry about long vacancies, often for a year at a time.

Many of the same skills will be required for each of these options. To be an investor of rental property, you must become the landlord and must obtain the necessary skills to fulfill this role.

2

SO YOU WANT TO BE A LANDLORD

JUST A LANDLORD?

If you own commercial or private property and agree to rent it to someone else, you become a landlord. Every person renting out property is a landlord of some type, whether it is a small one-man operation or a multimillion dollar operation with Donald Trump at the head.

Many people want to be a landlord to bring in the rent money every month and benefit from the increasing housing prices, but being a landlord is not that simple.

To be a landlord, you have to:

- Fill vacancies as quickly as possible.

- Know and follow the laws regarding rental properties.

- Make repairs on your properties as necessary.

- Provide a safe dwelling, also known as a habitable condition, for your tenants. At a minimum, you must ensure that the main systems in the house, such as electrical and plumbing, are properly maintained and maintain any common areas if you are renting a duplex, apartment unit, office complex, or other multi-tenant dwelling.

- Determine rent charges and collect those charges monthly.

- Find good tenants and keep them. You will have to screen your tenants carefully, looking for those who will treat your property with respect, pay their rent, and be free from criminal conduct.

- Deal with difficult tenants.

- Keep accurate records of applications, rent payments, agreements, notices, purchases, repairs, maintenance, and services.

- File taxes.

- Maintain insurance on the properties.

Though the drawbacks of becoming a landlord are many, so are the benefits. For instance, you can create a stream of income that supports your investment and may even provide you with monthly income for living expenses. While you earn this income, your investment will continue to appreciate as long as it is maintained properly, so you can see profits immediately and in the long-term.

To be a landlord, you have to determine whether the benefits of owning the property outweigh the risks and annoyances involved.

WHAT IS YOUR TYPE?

There are three main types of landlords: owner-occupant, absentee, and property manager. Determining which type you want to be will depend on your investment goals, your time, your knowledge, and your desire to be directly involved in the day-to-day operations of your rental properties.

Owner-Occupant Landlord

An owner-occupant landlord lives in the property being rented. An owner-occupant landlord situation is possible with any multi-tenant situation, such as an apartment building. If you choose to live on your investment property, you will find that your tenants expect immediate service when they have a problem. Being a landlord becomes a 24/7 job.

There are also many good aspects of being an owner-occupant. Even a responsible tenant is not as likely to keep the yard picked up or the unit clean as the owner of the property would. Rather than have an investment that is "out of sight, out of mind," owner-occupants constantly have the investment placed before them and will strive to keep up the conditions.

Absentee Landlord

This term has bad connotations, but it simply means the owner does not live on the premises. An absentee landlord can live one block away or several states away. Many absentee landlords check out their property on a regular basis and, although they cannot make immediate changes like an owner-occupant, they keep their property in good shape and deal with their tenants on a regular basis.

Investor Insight: It is true that some absentee landlords are truly absent except when it is time to collect a rent check. If you wish to be absent from the process, the best thing for you to do is to hire a property manager.

Property Manager

A property manager is a type of landlord who is paid by the owner of the property. For a set fee, the property manager can do the following:

- Rent or lease apartments
- Collect rents
- Find tenants
- Keep accounting records
- Hire contractors for repairs
- Return deposits
- Evict tenants

If you do not wish to be involved in the day-to-day workings of rental investments, this type of landlord arrangement may be right for you.

TEAM SPIRIT

Investing in real estate does not need to be a lone-wolf venture. You are going to do much better if you have a team you can trust. Team members will each bring their own expertise to the table to help you be successful.

Possible team members include:

1. **Bank broker or mortgage lender:** A broker can help you with many different financing options. A lender is the one who makes the loan decision and can give you pre-approval. It will be up to you to determine which you want on your team. You may decide that you want both.

Investor Insight: If you choose a mortgage lender, you may want to develop a relationship with someone in a small town community bank. Small banks are more flexible and can offer choices that larger banks do not have the decision-making power to give.

Whichever you choose, brokers and lenders are likely to have good relationships with realtors in your area, which brings us to the next team member on the list.

2. **Real estate agent:** An agent who is experienced in your area of investment is a good addition to your team. The agent will have access to the Multiple Listing Service and will know, often before you do, when something of interest to you is for sale.

   To find a good agent, ask around. Your banker may know of someone, but so may your friends. You can also go to the yellow pages and look at Web sites. Interview several agents until you feel comfortable with one. In the beginning, you may choose to work with three or four until you determine which one best suits your needs.

3. **Attorney:** You do not need just any attorney. You need a real estate attorney. You want someone who knows the real estate laws in your area and can help you close your deals quickly and easily. Since you will be buying rentals, you also will want your attorney to know about leases, tenant/landlord laws, evictions, and other items unique to rental property.

4. **Real Estate Accountant:** The IRS has hundreds of laws, deductions, and penalties that change every year. Having a good accountant who is well-versed in real estate finances is imperative.

5. **Real Estate Appraiser:** An appraiser is trained to give an estimate of the worth of a property. They will provide you with a detailed report that will be used by your mortgage lender to determine the amount of money that can be loaned on the property. A fair appraiser will know if you are getting a good deal and will get you the financing you need.

6. **Inspector:** Before purchasing a piece of property, you will want to have it inspected. Sometimes, a home that looks good to the novice is actually not. Structural defects, outdated wiring, and

poor plumbing may go unnoticed. An inspector can help you see what repairs need to be made and then you can determine whether the property meets your investment criteria.

7. **Contractor:** No matter what type of property you buy, there will be repairs to make either at the time of purchase or after a tenant leaves. These repairs may be large or small, but unless you are handy with tools and want to spend your time on maintenance, having a reliable contractor is a good addition to your team. In the beginning, you may need to try several different contractors until you find one who gives you reasonable and accurate quotes, gets the work done in a reasonable time, and is reliable.

Investor Insight: Having an inspector who is also a contractor can be quite valuable. This person will be able to tell you about the problems and the cost of repairs.

8. **Property Manager:** A final person you may want on your team is a property manager. Since this position requires full-time involvement in your investment business, the next section details what a property manager is and how to hire one.

YOU INVEST, THEY MANAGE

If you choose not to be involved in the day-to-day operations of your business, you will need to hire a property manager. You can either pay a company to do the work or hire an independent manager.

If you hire a company, you are contracting out the work; the management company is an expense but is not considered an employee. But if you hire an independent manager, you are hiring an employee and will be responsible for filing paperwork with the IRS and assuming responsibility for any actions taken by the manager.

Property Management Company

Here are a few things to look for when hiring a property management company:

1. **Fees:** Fees are derived in one of two ways — percentage fee or flat fee. The percentage fee is the most common and can be anywhere from 5 to 20 percent of the money your property brings in. You need to look for a reputable company that provides the most services for the least amount of money.

2. **Contact:** Consider whether the management company will be responsive to your calls, whether they use e-mail or have after-hour availability, and how quickly they will respond to you. You need to deal with a company that is personable and cares about you and your needs. Your investment is at stake, and you want someone who shows their concern toward you.

3. **Contract:** Find out whether there are charges or penalties to terminate your contract in case things are not working out.

4. **Property Maintenance:** There are several questions to ask a management company regarding maintenance:

   - Who does the maintenance on the property?

   - Do they have their own crew?

   - What do they charge you per hour for maintenance?

   - What kinds of repairs do they handle?

- What do they do if a repair comes about that they do not handle?

- How much will they spend without contacting you?

- Do they provide invoices and/or receipts for expenses due to repairs and maintenance?

Investor Insight: You will want to set a limit on what the management company may spend without contacting you. For many investors, $100 is a good set point.

5. **Statements:** Find out how often the company sends out income/expense statements. These are often sent monthly or quarterly, but monthly statements make it easier for you to determine whether the fees are what you expected and allow you to make quicker decisions concerning the management company.

6. **Tenant problems:** Find out how the management company handles evictions and whether this will be at an additional cost to you. Ask whether they have experienced legal counsel within their company to handle evictions.

7. **Yard work:** Determine whether yard work is part of the management company's responsibilities. Ask about the costs of yard work, landscaping, and snow removal.

8. **Reserves:** Management companies require that you put up a certain amount of money in reserve in case anything comes up quickly. You will want to find out how much money the company will require you to put into the reserve fund.

9. **Accounting:** Find out how often the management company sends a check to you and whether they put tenant deposits into an escrow account.

10. **Advertising:** Advertising will need to be done to fill vacancies. Find out where and how the management company advertises.

Investor Insight: According to the most recent surveys, 80 percent people hunting for a house to either buy or rent will look at options on the Internet first. This is an excellent resource for advertising.

You will also want to ask general questions such as:

- How many managers do they employ?

- How many properties do they manage?

- What types of rental properties do they focus on?

- How long have they been in business?

- Do they have referrals that you may contact?

Finding a good property management company will help you leave the day-to-day issues of real estate investing behind. You should constantly evaluate the relationship with your company and change companies as you feel necessary.

Independent Property Manager

When hiring an independent manager, you will need to determine what their job will entail.

- Will they select tenants?

- Will they resolve day-to-day problems?

- Will they maintain the property?

- Will they hire contractors?

- Will they make small repairs themselves?

- Will they collect rent?

- Will they evict tenants?

You will have to determine how much you plan to pay your employee. This is the same as it is with a management company — you have several options. You can give your employee a salary, pay by the hour, or pay a percentage.

If you have a multi-tenant property, you will also need to determine whether the property manager will live on the property. While common, this practice is not a necessity. Many real estate investors who hire a property manager include free rent for a unit as part of a managers salary.

As you interview potential employees, you will want to look at their previous experience and, if required by state law, whether the candidate possesses a current license. You will also want to check their references. The manager will need to be familiar with Fair Housing Laws, basic landlord-tenant laws, accounting practices, the Internet, and basic maintenance.

Investor Insight: Do not simply collect their references. Check them out. Ask questions about their experience, personality, and style. If you just ask whether they were a good employee, you are likely to get a yes answer but no real information.

Some questions you may consider asking during an interview to hire an independent property manager include:

- Tell me about your past experience. What did you like most about your last job? What did you like the least?

- Do you have experience collecting rent?

- Do you have experience doing general repairs?

- What kinds of problems have you resolved in the past? How did you resolve them?

- What about this job interests you?

After you interview the applicant and check their references, you will need to check credit history and background. Your property manager will be handling money with no direct supervision. Someone with poor personal finances may not handle rent money correctly or may be more inclined to steal. The checks give information on character, reputation, and lifestyle.

Investor Insight: You must obtain the applicant's consent to check their credit and background by using a form with their signature and date. If they refuse these checks, do not consider them for the position.

Depending on your needs, hiring an independent property manager may be best for your investment goals. Whether you hire a company or an individual, you are the owner of the property and it is up to you to do what is best for your tenants. If you do not like the management of your property. It is in your best interest.

After you understand the role of a landlord and make your decision to become one, it is time to think about the property you will buy. In Chapter 3, we will explore how to find the right rental home for you.

3

SEEK AND YE SHALL FIND

As you look at rental properties, you will notice that the process takes plenty of time, a network of people, and knowledge. Jumping in without the proper base is a recipe for disaster.

WAIT, DO NOT SEEK YET

Before you even begin looking at a property, there are some things you must consider first.

Look at the Time

Consider how long you plan to own a rental property. The longer you own, the more appreciation you will earn in the end, but you will also be investing in more repairs, maintenance, and improvements.

If you plan to keep a home for 10 years and the home is five years old, you most likely will not have to put on a new roof or buy new appliances. On the other hand, if you plan to keep the home for 20 years, you are likely to have to replace the roof and the major appliances. If you only plan to keep a home for a short time, you will want to buy a property that will not need major repairs unless you believe you can recoup the cost of those repairs.

Another thing to consider is the appreciation of the home. If you keep a home for 20 years, the appreciation on the property will be high. If you plan to sell in five years, you will need to make more money on the minimal appreciation in that time and a bigger annual return through higher rents to make the purchase worthwhile.

Investor Insight: For most small investors, long-term property investing is the wisest choice because it allows them to remain unscathed during market dips.

Networks Count

Developing a network is a good way to find properties that are available. Trying to find one on your own is not as easy because the good ones may be snatched up quickly by those "in the know."

As you get started, you will want to join local landlord associations, property owner associations, real estate groups, and chamber groups. These groups will help you find out what is for sale. As you become more known in these circles, people with deals will come looking for you instead of you having to do all the searching.

Another method is to approach a landlord directly to see if they want to sell their property. You will be surprised by the number of landlords who are ready to get out of the business or find your offer appealing.

Money Matters

You are going to need a loan to get started on your real estate investing venture. To get an excellent loan, you will need an excellent credit rating. If your credit rating is poor, you will need bigger down payments and will receive higher interest rates.

Additionally, when applying for a loan for a rental unit, the bank wants to see the financial balance sheet. If your credit is poor, this balance sheet will have to be much stronger than the normal requirement.

To get a better credit rating, pay down credit cards and consumer debt and pay all your bills on time. Doing these two things will increase your credit score in a matter of six to 12 months.

You will also need a cash reserve beyond the required down payment when buying the property. This cash reserve is for unexpected repairs, maintenance, and vacancies. The money you owe the bank is due whether you have a tenant or not. If your unit is vacant for two months, you need to have the money to make the mortgage payment without a tenant's rent.

Investor Insight: The rule of thumb is that you set aside at least one month's rent for each unit. You may also consider having a line of credit to cover large costs.

In the Know

When it comes to real estate investing, knowledge is imperative.

If you overpay, you will have a much tougher time recouping your initial investment, and you will never make as much as you could have if you had made a better deal. Real estate investing has to be practical. If you let your emotions take over, you will be blind to bad deals. Stick to the numbers. Falling in love with a piece of property without looking at recouping the investment is investor suicide.

Ensuring that rental income will cover your costs is key. These costs include:

- Taxes
- Insurance

- Maintenance and Repairs
- Vacancy rate
- Mortgage payment on the property

Investor Insight: The typical vacancy rate is 5 percent. If you have one unit for 12 months and multiply that by 5 percent, you can expect to have the unit empty half a month each year or one month every two years.

Now that you know the basics, the goal of finding an investment property can be realized.

Been There, Done That

Dawn Cook shares what she looks for in a rental property and why:

Price is first for us, then area, and then the condition of the place.

Price is always most important to us. If we do not get a good price, then it might not be worth it to us to rent it out. We always keep in mind the option of selling, so we need a nice margin of profit in that area as well. I feel a property should always be able to pay for itself, plus extra for our pocket and for any future problem that may arise.

Location is key. If the property is in an undesirable area, you may have a problem obtaining renters and keeping them. Finally, we look at the physical shape of the property. We do not want to put much work into the place to get it ready to rent. It is a blessing to put a for rent sign up and start the ad in the paper on the day of closing.

We prefer one bedroom units because they are for one to two people. This way, we do not have to deal with multiple people in and out regarding wear and tear on the property. It also eliminates multiple vehicles and we get, in our opinion, more money in return.

We see it as this: The more people in a property, the higher likelihood of problems and issues that will take up our time and possibly our money. In the past, we have had excellent experiences with one bedroom places. They are quickly rented with minimal headaches.

LOCATION, LOCATION, LOCATION

If you have been around real estate in any way, you have heard that the three most important factors when buying real estate are location, location, location. Location is important when dealing with rental properties as well. Without the proper location, you will not be able to earn enough tenant income to pay your monthly bills.

The problem lies in the fact that there is no one right location. It depends on your particular area and your particular investment goals. There are many things to consider when searching for a rental property to purchase.

If you want to invest in a busy city, units that are close to public transportation and city amenities, such as restaurants and theaters, will be in the right location. On the other hand, if you are buying in a suburban neighborhood, a unit near a shopping center and local park and in a good school district makes more sense.

If you are buying vacation rentals, a home on the beach is preferable to one a block from the ocean. A lakefront property will bring you higher rents than one that simply has a view of the lake.

If your rentals will be for working families, buying property in areas with many jobs or in easy commuting distance of a bigger city will be essential. Working families will also want grocery stores nearby, local daycare centers, and activities such as soccer and scouting.

When checking out the location, you will want to walk through the area on several different occasions and at several different times of the day. While you are looking around, ask yourself whether you would feel comfortable living there as a renter.

Other questions to consider are:

- How is the neighborhood kept up? Are the homes taken care of and is the yard work being done?

- What kind of amenities are in the area? Look for shopping centers, grocery stores, parks, jogging trails, restaurants, and access to local transit systems such as buses or trains.

- Is the school system good? Does the school offer after-school care?

- Are there sidewalks, parks, and playgrounds for children to play?

- Does the property have a fenced yard for children and pets?

- How easy is it to access the interstate or other main routes into and out of town?

- Is the property close to you?

As you start your rental business, having your properties close at hand will make the whole process easier. If you look for properties near your home, you will be better able to answer all the questions about the neighborhood. It will also be easier to find the help you need, such as repair work, by using someone you already know and trust.

HOUSES, APARTMENTS, CONDOS, OH MY

In addition to location, you must consider the type of property you wish to purchase. City dwellers want to be near city amenities, but they also want something easy to take care of. Those in the city do not tend to want yards. Condominiums or apartments would fit this description.

If you are considering buying homes for the working class, you need to think about families. Most families want three bedrooms, a garage, and a yard, suggesting single-family homes or a duplex. Single renters or young couples are looking for two bedrooms and often do not care as much about a yard, suggesting a duplex, a townhome, or an apartment building.

Even if you decide to buy single-family homes, there are more decisions to make. Do you want one, two, three, or four bedrooms? Do you want a garage, a carport, or no protection for a vehicle? Do you want a yard? Will the yard be fenced? Do you want a deck or patio? Do you want one story or two? Do you want a home with a basement? What about a workshop or storage shed?

To figure out these details, you need to figure out who your tenants will be by looking at your area and examining the market.

HOW MUCH?

How much you are willing to spend on your investment property will depend on your credit, your down payment, your reserve cash, and the amount the bank will loan you. You can determine what a bank will loan you by getting pre-approved. If you have to put 5 percent down and the bank loans you up to $175,000, you can only look at homes that are $175,000 or less — as long as you have $8,750 for the down payment and at least one month's rent. The hard part is determining if the property you are looking at is a good buy.

A good rule of thumb is to look for a house at or below the median price range of a neighborhood. The median price range means that half the houses sold are more expensive and half are less expensive than the property you are considering. You can find the median home price by asking any real estate agent in your area. Median sale prices differ widely from region to region, and even from neighborhood to neighborhood.

By choosing homes that are at or below the median price, you are providing a more affordable home to your tenant while putting out less investment money to purchase the property.

Smaller houses also have higher returns because you can get a higher rate per square foot than for larger homes. For instance, if you have a 1,000 square foot home and can rent it for $1,000, you are receiving $1 per square foot. On the other hand, if you have a 2,000 square foot home and can rent it for $1,500, you are only getting $0.75 per foot.

DO NOT JUDGE A BOOK BY ITS COVER

You should never judge a home by its outside appearance. A home may look good on the outside, but may really be in poor physical condition. Conversely, a home may look like it is in horrendous shape, but it really only needs some tender-loving care.

The best way to determine the real physical condition of a property is to have it inspected by a professional. The physical condition that you are willing to accept will be determined by your investment objectives. Some people want to only make minor repairs, while others look for homes that are in distress.

Investor Insight: Ask to attend the walkthrough with the inspector. Watching how he inspects and what he looks for will give you tips on how to do your own preliminary inspections in the future.

Initially, you should look for homes that need few repairs. These homes will bring you the most profit because you will not need to spend much time on repairs before bringing in a rent check. You will also be able to maximize your ROI because your investment will be low compared to the money you will receive.

Even if you are willing to make repairs, avoid homes that have:

- **Weak or bad foundations** — A home with a bad foundation will have large cracks in the drywall, larger than normal separations in brick mortar, and doorjambs and window casings out of alignment.

- **Moisture problems** — If a basement has a moisture problem, you will have to deal with mold, which can get extremely expensive.

- **Old plumbing**

- **Out-of-date electrical wiring**

TODAY OR TOMORROW?

It is always the right time to buy.

If you know what you want out of a rental property, have your finances in order, have a network in place, and have done your research, you are ready to begin. It is possible to research and analyze yourself into inactivity and never get started.

There is no perfect deal — there are only good deals.

CAN YOU MAKE IT WORK?

Knowing how much you can charge for rent is one of the keys to making a property work. If you cannot charge enough, you will not break even.

Finding the going rate for rental properties in your area is a simple task. Check newspaper ad listings for apartments and homes in your area. Check out the number of bedrooms, baths, and other amenities. If the advertisement does not list a price, call and ask. Knowing what other landlords are charging for similar properties will help you establish what tenants will pay for your property.

Just because you are renting a three-bedroom, two-bath house does not mean that it will bring in the same rent as another in your area. You have to look at the property as a whole and ask yourself these questions:

1. Does my property offer things to the tenant that other properties do not?

2. Is my property closer to shopping centers or main arteries?

3. Is my property in a better school district?

4. Is my property in a better neighborhood?

Honestly answering these questions will help you establish a rental rate, and then you can determine whether that rate will let you break even. If the answer is no, then the deal is not a good one.

Now that you know the criteria for finding the right rental home, you need to begin the hunt. In Chapter 4, we will explore the ins and outs of finding the right property.

CASE STUDY: JANE

Jane is a small investor in Florida. She watched her parents invest in real estate during her growing up years and learned much from them. First and foremost, she learned that knowing your market is essential.

"I was aware of the market. I think of real estate as my hobby. I love watching the market. My parents always told me to find something you like to do and then find a way to make money with it. Whenever I see a sign for sale in my neighborhood, or close by, I will call up. I do not have any intention of purchasing. I simply want to know what they are asking. You see, you listen, you read articles on real estate. and keep yourself appraised on the market."

CASE STUDY: JANE

Jane got the itch and nearly bought a condo, but a trusted lender whom she had built a relationship with helped her see that it was not a good investment. "Thanks to him, I did not make a bad mistake. A good lender is important to have on your side."

She abandoned the deal on the property, but became disheartened and was not actively looking until a year later. She found something in the city, though she lived in a more rural area. She found a good property but was apprehensive.

"The gut feeling goes a long way. I was not comfortable. I was happy, but something just did not feel right. Certain factors were not right for us as buyers. My parents always warned me that buying a home far away can be difficult. There were many hassles unless you wanted to use a management company, and I knew that I wanted to do the landlording myself.

"How would I start renting the place? I would have to show up an hour away just to show it. The property made good sense in terms of money, but it was not without much time and effort. I convinced my husband that we had to cancel it. He was disappointed."

For Jane, finding areas that are similar to her own neighborhood makes determining whether a property is a good one much easier. Since she is more like her eventual tenants, she can answer questions about how her tenant would feel about living there and whether the house is close enough to the amenities her tenant will want.

To find properties in her area, Jane looks in many different locations, such as:

- **Realtor.com**
- Local newspaper
- Flyers
- **Craigslist.org**
- Web sites providing MLS listings
- Bulletin announcements at the grocery store, bank, or other local area

She also watches every for sale sign in her neighborhood and will check each one out. Her research paid off after turning down the property in the city.

"We already had a locked in rate, so I started looking at everything in our local market. Because I had already done all the research in my own area, I had a contract submitted for a house five minutes from my own in one week. By going just a few miles too far beyond my area of expertise a possible good deal could have been a bad one."

CASE STUDY: JANE

Jane believes that, as long as you have done your research and know your market, there is never a bad time to buy. Timing is about finding the right bargain, not about market dips or time of the year. These issues may affect when you sell, but should not enter the equation when you buy. If you are financially able, the time is right.

Jane, though an absentee landlord, is a hands-on landlord. She and her husband find their own tenants, deal with tenant issues, maintain the property, and keep their own records. Larger projects will be contracted out to those who have more expertise.

In addition to having a good lender and a good contractor, Jane believes having a good attorney is crucial. "I found a good attorney in Miami and miss her because I do not have one at the moment. I talked with my realtor, who recommended a good attorney. I used them once and like the company, but I did not click. Finding someone you click with and who can be the muscle standing behind you on a deal is a great feeling."

Each landlord has a different set of standards when finding a good tenant. For Jane, her tenants must have an excellent credit history for the past two years and good references from their last landlord. To her, the key to successful investing, after you find the right property, is finding good tenants.

"I was looking at a Web site, and it gave some good advice. As the potential renter pulls up, notice the condition of their car. How they keep their car is going to be similar to how they are going to treat your property. The article also suggested that you notice whether they wipe their feet before entering the house. I do this as I interview possible tenants. It eliminates many right away."

What will Jane do if she gets a bad tenant? "Find a good attorney – fast." She says you need to know the eviction process inside and out, before you need it.

Jane did not realize how good it was to invest in property until she did it for herself. "If only people understood that even if you have to pay the mortgage now and again, you get so much more for the same amount of money."

READY OR NOT, HERE I COME

Now that you are ready to buy your first home, let us discuss where you should look.

Finding a rental property is easy; you just have to know where to look. In this chapter, we will explore seven ways to find the right rental home.

READ ALL ABOUT IT

One of the easiest ways to find a home for sale is by checking the classified section of your local newspaper.

Ads in the newspaper can be created by real estate agents or For Sale By Owners (FSBOs). It does not matter who put the ad in the paper. What matters is whether the home for sale meets your criteria.

One way to find a good property is to look for certain words in the advertisements. Some phrases to watch out for might be:

- Investment opportunity
- Great rental property
- Seller is motivated
- Seller is flexible
- Starter home

For example:

> *FSBO, LAKE TILLERY, A-Frame 3BR fixer-upper, annual views Moro Mtn and Lake, $147,000.*

Or:

> *Reduced! Home for Sale! Renovated 2BR/1BA, ½ ac with detached garage. New kitchen and floors. Covered front porch, Large back deck. Fenced back yard.*

Or:

> *MOTIVATED SELLER 2,700 sq ft brick house in Robbins. 4 or 5BR/1BA, basement, hardwood floors, Needs some TLC. Priced below tax value. $91,000.*

Homes that have these descriptions are often in older, more established neighborhoods. These neighborhoods are a good place to find a rental home.

Call the number and look at the home. If the advertiser is a real estate agent, then even if you decide that the home is not for you, you have made a contact. Talk with them about what you need. They may be able to help you or put you in contact with a realtor in their office who specializes in investment properties.

Been There, Done That

Debbie Malone bought a four family unit for $30,000 five years ago that was a HUD foreclosure. It was not listed correctly. Instead of showing the property as a multi-tenant unit, it showed it as a two-bedroom single family dwelling. In actuality, it had two units with two bedrooms, an efficiency unit, and an unfinished unit. Even with the three units rented, it was a cash cow. Debbie said, "We would say 'moo' every time we drove by. We sold it two years ago for $92,000."

You can also place your own ad in the "real estate wanted" section. This type of advertising does not need to be costly. All you are trying to do is let people know exactly what you are looking for.

Your ad needs to be specific. If you only want three or four bedroom homes with two or more baths, be sure to say so. There is no need wasting your time on homes that do not meet this criterion.

For example:

> *Seeking apartment buildings to purchase. Wanting 120 to 150 units. Must be within ten miles of downtown. Call 1-555-555-1234.*

Or you can be more specific:

> *Looking for single family home or town home in the $500,000 to $650,000 range. Minimum 3 bedrooms and 2 baths. Square footage between 1,500 and 2,100 square feet. Home not older than 20 years. In excellent school district. In the following areas: San Jose, Cupertino, Sunnyvale, Santa Clara. Call 1-555-555-1234.*

REAL ESTATE MAGAZINES

Other good sources of homes are the local real estate magazines. Almost every area publishes a magazine, either weekly or monthly, that shows homes for sale. Some areas have more than one magazine. You can find these magazines outside real estate offices, drug stores, grocery stores, and local gathering places.

These magazines are put out by real estate agents or a group of agents. They list their houses on one or two pages, give their contact information, and tell you why you should purchase your home from them. This information may give you some insight into the type of realtor who has the property for sale.

If you see a home that interests you, call the agent. Although most agents in these publications deal with traditional retail housing, you may get lucky and find an agent who specializes in investment properties. Even if they do not, they may have a property that will suit your needs or be able to refer to someone who does specialize in investment properties.

> **Investor Insight:** Real estate magazines can be a good source of real estate related products and services. Such services include real estate agents, mortgage companies, appraisers, surveyors, title companies, real estate attorneys, and insurance companies.

GETTING WEB SAVVY

For many, the best way to find a property is by searching online. You can search online simply by using a search engine like Google with the words "homes for sale Raleigh, NC," for example. You will have a large list of sites to choose from. These sites can either be specialized sites that list properties from many areas or more local sites, often run by a specific agent. The best part about searching online is that many sites will give you automatic e-mail updates when new homes are added to the database that meet your specific criteria.

The best known site for this kind of search is **www.realtor.com**, hosted by the National Association of Realtors. This site gets all of its information from the MLS listings, so no FSBO homes will be listed.

The other way to find homes online is to read the online classifieds instead of the newspaper classifieds. This method can save you time if the site allows you to choose criteria before searching the properties.

Been There, Done That

Dawn Cook uses a variety of methods to locate her investment properties:

"I found most of them FSBO. I feel the best ways to find rental properties are keeping a sharp eye out for good deals by checking the local MLS Web site often, watching for FSBOs, and asking questions of people whenever they mention a property for sale or about to go on sale. This keeps you informed and up-to-date on potential properties in an area that you may want to purchase a rental property. I avoid the paper because today things get sold quickly, and I do not feel that the paper gives enough information like the Internet or a drive by of a FSBO."

ASK A PRO

Talking with someone in the business is a good idea. The type of agent you are looking for is someone who:

- Works full-time
- Is Internet savvy
- Loves their job
- Uses new technologies
- Has handled investment properties in the past

Your chosen agent should be in the day-to-day loop of his business so that he can bring you new properties as they become available. A good agent will always be on the lookout for a good deal on a property that meets your specifications. You will have to share with them exactly what you are looking for, otherwise they will bring you deals that will waste your time and theirs.

Real estate agents, by law, have to act in your best interest. They are required to do everything possible to help you find a good deal and make sound investment decisions. They can provide you with up-to-date market information, such as comparable sales data, to help make your decisions more accurate.

There is no need to be limited to one real estate agent. Realtor A may be well-known among some circles, and Realtor B among others. Although there may be some overlap, each will have sources unknown to the other. Having a broader reach is beneficial to your investment goals.

CASE STUDY: AZIZ ABDUR-RA'OOF

Aziz is a realtor in Maryland, but he does not limit his investment purchases to those he finds on his own. "A realtor mentioned something to me and I started looking at the area and did much research on my own. The home was a FSBO. I talked with the owners and decided it was a good deal. "Why did not the realtor who gave me the lead take the deal? I assume that the house did not meet his investing criteria, nor did it meet the criteria of his real estate business. For me, opportunity and favorable terms make a good deal."

Aziz also looks at foreclosures as a source of investment properties, but he cautions that this may be something to avoid if you do not know foreclosure law or do not have a trusted attorney who does.

On the note of foreclosures and property owners in distress, Aziz gives a caution to investors. "We are in the people business. If someone does not want their home anymore or cannot afford to stay in their home anymore, this will make a good deal for you. However, it is imperative that you do not take advantage of them. The Golden Rule applies: Do not do something to someone that you would not want done to you."

One of Aziz's best experiences with a purchase came about with an owner who simply needed to get out of his home. "When I spoke directly to the owner, he threw out a number. The number seemed high to me, so I used a technique that I learned. I asked him what amount he would be willing to sell his home for in cash in seven days and then I shut up. There will be silence. Wait until they start to speak. He wanted out with a quick sale. I wanted the house. I believe in win-win. In his case, it was not as much about price as it was about timing. He wanted to move on with his life and a quick closing met that need. I ended up getting the house for less than his original number, but it was a fair price for him."

For Aziz, determining whether a property is right is as simple as running the analysis.

CASE STUDY: AZIZ ABDUR-RA'OOF

If it meets your criteria and the numbers make sense, then the property is right. If you know your criteria, you can determine pretty quickly whether the property will work.

For instance, if you focus on homes that are in the entry level phase, you will see those that pop up that meet this criterion. Since you have already researched the area, you know whether it is a good price, and you know the rental prices in the area. You can look at the school system and other amenities like proximity to jobs or big cities.

When Aziz decides on a home, he looks closely at the physical shape of the home. If problems are merely cosmetic, he does not worry too much. Larger issues, like plumbing, take more consideration and he determines whether it will fit into his budget and the acquisition price.

"If I think I can get it done in a reasonable amount of time and with a reasonable amount of money, I will do it. I look at it as a way to get it at a lower price. The caveat is that I am sure I have the people to come in to do the repairs immediately."

Aziz advises that you put together a team, though he suggests that it can happen over time. "I like talking to other realtors who are investors and other investors. I am always looking to see if there is someone out there who can help me, like a painter, an insurance agent, or a carpet layer. I am always networking."

Although he is capable of a few minor repairs, Aziz feels that it is in his best financial interest to get a professional to do the work for him. He assesses what needs to be fixed and then hires out. He says that it is important to watch for trends. For instance, carpet is no longer "in" so he often replaces worn carpet with hardwood floors.

The more you buy and fix up, the easier it becomes. "Once you fix one up, you have a template in your mind and do the same thing to all the properties. Tubs, paint, and carpet are the same for each similar unit. It allows me to get the house ready for rent as quickly as possible. I just stay out of the way and let others do their work."

Finally, Aziz has a word about leases — use one. "A lease is necessary because we forget. We can make a minor mistake that can turn out to be a major issue. If you have everything written down, you and your tenants can reference back to it. Not using a lease is setting yourself up for failure."

For Aziz, real estate is a good investment whether the market is up or down. It is not a get rich quick scheme, but if you stick to your plan, you can eventually realize your investment goals.

CASE STUDY: AZIZ ABDUR-RA'OOF

Aziz Abdur-Ra'oof
"From A to Z the Right Catch in Real Estate"
Keller Williams® Realty Centre
6230 Old Dobbin Lane, Suite 150
Columbia, MD 21045
240-994-9553

SCOUT IT OUT

A scout is someone who can find a house for you that meets your investment criteria. Anyone can be a scout. All it takes is an understanding of what you are looking for and the ability to provide you with leads that include the appropriate information.

Such information includes:

- Location of the home
- Condition of the home

- Asking price
- Condition of the neighborhood

- Seller's terms
- Any timing requirements

- Degree of urgency
- Comparable sales data

A good scout will always be looking out for houses that meet your needs. They then pass this information on to you so you can make a final decision. If you purchase the home, then your scout will get monetary compensation known as a finder's fee. Finder's fees are often in the neighborhood of $500, but are only paid when the information leads to an actual purchase of a property.

Using a scout will broaden the scope of your search and help you find the best deals.

FSBOS

Another way to find a home is by looking to those selling their own homes. These sellers are known as FSBOs. Those selling their home on their own often have a sign in the front yard or have listed their property in the paper or online.

Checking out these signs and ads is a good way to find properties that may go unseen by agents or real estate magazines. If not caught at the right time, you can even miss an FSBO home in the paper.

> **Investor Insight:** Most FSBO sellers turn to a realtor within 60 to 90 days of putting their home on the market. You may be able to get a good deal during this time period, as they are more likely to give you the discount rather than pay a realtor's fees.

IT IS NOT WHO YOU KNOW BUT WHO KNOWS YOU

Getting your name out in your community as a real estate investor will help you find properties, and affiliating with a professional organization is a good way to get your name out there. Professional organizations include local groups, such as the chamber of commerce, or a local real estate investor's club. It can also mean a regional or national organization, such as the National Association of Home Builders.

> **Investor Insight:** Joining at least two clubs will help you gain the type of network needed to be successful in real estate investing.

You can find investment clubs near you by going to:

www.realestatepromo.com

www.real-estate-online.com

You can also find these associations by looking in the yellow pages or doing an Internet search.

Been There, Done That

Marilynn Currie of Canada tells this story of a friendship that spawned an investment empire:

"My dentist is the millionaire next door. Unassuming and friendly, he lives in the family home that he bought when his children were small. He drives a small car that gets him from home to work and, on good days, he bicycles.

"As he said to me while working on my teeth, 'My wife says I have the same underwear that I wore in graduate school.'

"Way back in the late '70s, he had as a patient a young Realtor who needed major dental work. And as he was a young man growing his practice, they struck up a great friendship. Thereafter, the Realtor would schedule his appointments just before the lunch hour and then with the two hour window of time, they were off looking at investment properties. With a little bit of financial wizardry, he often bought two homes a week.

"Now, 30 or so years later, his investment properties are all over the world, from Canada to China to the U.S.A. — 55 homes and counting. He recently bought a defunct ice cream plant and sells his major output to Costco. Three of his children are now in dental school in Philadelphia, so he bought two townhouses and his kids rent the rooms out to fellow students. He says when tuition is due, 'If there is not enough scholarship money, I just sell one of my homes, and pay the tuition.'

"I asked him what his secret was of such success. He said, 'Choose a Realtor you can trust, have a great banker, make sure your rent for the properties pays all the costs plus repairs, and choose your tenants carefully.'

"And who runs the business? His wife of course. They keep it all in the family."

Using the methods found in this chapter, you will be able to find properties that will make a good start on your investment portfolio. In Chapter 5, we will explore methods of determining whether the investment property makes monetary sense.

WILL THE PROPERTY MAKE MONEY

Cash flow is essential, so checking the numbers is imperative. The property must show that it will make money.

To keep from paying too much, determine the value of the property. If you have a car or a rare coin, you can look in a book to determine its value. There is no book to look in to determine the value of real estate.

It is essential that you learn to estimate the value for yourself. This process is not difficult, especially since you can find much of the needed information on the Internet.

Market value is the most likely price a property could bring in a competitive market. Do not confuse a home's market value with its tax assessed value.

The tax assessed value is determined when someone in the tax department of your city or county looks at the property and determines a value. Depending on your area, a tax assessment can be as little as 70 percent of the fair market value. The appraised value is determined by a licensed appraiser and is based on the price of similar homes in the area.

There are three main methods used by real estate investors to determine the value of property. The rest of this chapter is devoted to these methods.

COMPARATIVE MARKET ANALYSIS

This method is the one most used to determine whether the price you are paying is the right price.

> **Investor Insight:** For a rental property, you will need to know whether you will make money based on the rent. Therefore, a Comparative Market Analysis (CMA) is a good place to start.

A CMA bases a property value on surrounding properties that have recently sold. These properties are similar in size, amenities, and features. To be accurate, the comps must be based on properties that were not sold at low prices or using financing not available to the average buyer.

A good CMA will address the following items:

Location: You should first look at properties that are in the same neighborhood as the one you plan to buy. Differences in location can be difficult to adjust for. Do not use comp houses that are outside the school district or in another town.

Time: Use comp data that is no more than six months old. If it is a slow market, you may have to go back further. Also, use only closed sales. The price could change on pending sales.

Housing Style: Look at houses that are the same style as the one you are looking at. Also, look at the zoning of the area. Do not compare houses that are in different zoning, such as a residential to a commercial.

Size: Be sure your comp has a similar house and lot size.

Rooms: Try to find homes similar in the number of bedrooms and baths and have the same kind of family room, garage, utilities, or basement.

Condition: Condition is best assessed by a drive-by and can only be accounted for by looking on the outside. You can supplement what you see by the data on the MLS. Look for things like maintenance free exteriors, flooring, new kitchens and baths, and other improvements.

Age: It is best to compare homes that are of a similar age. If the only homes available for comps are far different, you will have to adjust.

> **Investor Insight:** Using the figure of $1,000 per year difference is a good way to adjust for age. If a comp home is 20 years old and your home is only 8 years old, you can add $12,000 to the value of your home.

You can get the information you need from any area real estate agent. Most agents can even send the comps to you online.

INCOME METHOD

When you have determined whether you can buy the property at a good price, it is time to see whether the property will make you any money. You will need to learn about Capitalization Rates and Gross Rent Multipliers.

The Capitalization Rate (cap rate) is determined by dividing the property's net operating income by its purchase price. The income you make will have to pay for the mortgage, insurance, taxes, and repairs. A cap rate below 8 percent will erase your profits and begin to cost you money.

For instance, if you find a piece of property for $150,000 and it generates $1,000 per month, the cap rate would be 8 percent. (Net income is $1,000 times 12 months, so the cap rate is $12,000 divided by $150,000.) If you had to pay $175,000 for the same piece of property, your cap rate would be 7 percent — too low to be considered a good deal.

The Gross Rent Multiplier (GRM) is the sales price divided by the monthly gross income of the property. In the case of the $150,000 property above, the GRM would be 150. Now, take the Gross Rent Multiplier of 150 and multiply it by the gross yearly rent of $12,000 to get a figure of $180,000. According to the GRM method, the home is worth $30,000 more than you are paying for it.

Of course, you are assuming that $1,000 is the right rent to charge and it will pay the bills and provide a profit. Let us see if $1,000 will do that.

First, you will want to know the mortgage payment, your insurance, and your property taxes. This information can be obtained from your loan officer.

For the next several categories, you will need information from the owner. If they used the property as a rental before, you will want their Schedule E, their income and expense statement, and all the rental agreements from the past year. Additionally, you will want utility bills and repair and capital improvement bills from the last year. If the property has never been rented in the past, you will only be able to get the utility and capital improvement bills.

Mortgage Payment	$_____
Insurance Payment	$_____
Monthly Taxes	$_____
Monthly Maintenance	$_____
Monthly Repairs	$_____
Monthly Utility	$_____
Monthly Admin Cost	$_____
Other Monthly Debt	$_____
Monthly Vacancy Reserve	$_____
Monthly ROI	$_____
Total Expenses	$_____

After you have collected this information from the owner, you will want to determine the monthly maintenance expense. This includes things like trash removal, yard work, snow removal, and minor repairs. If you have a figure for the year, divide it by 12 to get the monthly amount.

Next, you need to figure the repairs amount. This is money you will need to set aside for larger repairs such as the roof or the heating unit. You will need to look at the average life expectancy of the:

- Roof
- Electrical system
- Plumbing
- HVAC unit
- Appliances
- Exterior paint
- Vinyl siding

Determine how many of these items you will need to replace over the next five years and add up the price of the replacement. Divide by 60 (five years is 60 months) to get the monthly amount you should have in reserve.

Next you need to find out utility costs for a year and then divide by 12 to get a monthly cost. If you will not be paying the utilities for the property, simply put a zero in this category.

Administrative costs can be found by looking at the owner's Schedule E and income/expense statement. These are such things as advertising, accounting and legal services, office supplies, and even gas used to go to and from the property.

If you plan to do a rehab or other large improvement, figure the total and divide by 12 to find "other" debt.

You will then want to set aside a vacancy reserve. This is money needed to pay the mortgage when the unit is vacant. Most investors suggest having 1 percent. Divide this amount by 12 to get the monthly reserve.

Finally, to determine the ROI you are seeking, seek out the counsel of your accountant. A 5 to 8 percent return is considered good. When this number is determined, divide it by 12 to provide your monthly investment return.

Now add up all those numbers to find your total monthly expenses. Divide that number by the number of units and you have the average per unit.

Mortgage Payment	$727
Insurance Payment	$100
Monthly Taxes	$75
Monthly Maintenance	$50
Monthly Repairs	$50
Monthly Utility	$0
Monthly Admin Cost	$20
Other Monthly Debt	$0
Monthly Vacancy Reserve	$125
Monthly ROI	$200
Total Expenses	**$1,347**
Rental Price Per Unit	**$1,347**

Now let us get back to our example. The property you wish to buy is $150,000 for a single family home. You will put down $30,000 so your mortgage will be for $120,000 at 6.11 percent for 30 years. You also want an 8 percent ROI. The other figures were obtained from the owner of the property and the need for about $3,000 in repairs over the next five years.

To pay the bills and earn your desired ROI, you will have to charge $1,350 per month in rent. Whether that amount is a good deal depends on the area. If the homes in the area that are like yours rent for about the same, the number works. If, on the other hand, the properties rent for $1,000, you are not likely to find a renter for your unit at $1,350. Even if you wanted a zero ROI, you will be losing $150 a month by offering the home at $1,000 per month.

Been There Done That

Chris Lingquist has this to say about determining whether a property is a good investment:

"The first property I bought, I forgot to figure in the Homeowner's Association fees and a reasonable vacancy and repair fund. That is not the fault of real estate investing. That is the fault of someone not knowing what he is doing. Most of my bad stories start and stop with something that should have been under my control."

REPLACEMENT COST METHOD

This method estimates how much it would cost you to replace the structures on the property without the cost of the land. These costs are determined by dividing the total number of square feet in a building by the per square foot construction cost of a new building.

For example, a 2,000 square foot home, in an area where $175 per square foot is typical for new construction, would cost $350,000. Therefore, if the home was selling for less than $350,000, the replacement cost method would suggest that it is a good deal.

You can find out the replacement cost by calling an insurance broker. In the case of our $150,000 home, using the replacement cost of $110 per square foot on the 1,500 square foot home would give us a value of $165,000, suggesting that this would be a good deal.

Different methods tell you different things. The comp model and replacement model deal strictly with the cost of the property. In both, the property is a good deal. When looking at the income related models, the CAP rate looks good, but the GRM shows that the property cannot sustain itself based on the rents in the neighborhood.

As someone merely wishing to buy a home for their own, this house represents a good deal. But as an investor, you would want to pass.

CASE STUDY: STEVE ALEFF

For Steve Aleff, an investor in Duluth, Minnesota, it is easy to know whether a property is a good one. He looks at the "bedroom number and quality based on the price of the property. I allow $300 per bedroom in rent times the number of bedrooms at 80 percent times 100. That will give you the most you can afford to pay for a property and have positive net cash flow with a 20 percent down payment on the purchase. For example, a six bedroom house at $300/bedroom = $1,800 x 80 percent = $1,440. Multiply this by 100 and you get $144,000. That is the maximum price I would be willing to spend on this property."

CASE STUDY: STEVE ALEFF

This formula will not work for everyone in all areas because rents differ so much. Instead, you might want to simply put in the figure for the rent and then do the rest of the math.

For Steven, pristine is not a condition of purchase. "All of the properties I acquired had a story or issue. We look for situations that will put us in a position to acquire the properties at values that fit our model. These situations include death, estate, relocation, job change, moving to assisted living, empty nesters, or bankruptcy. We rely on involvement in the community both by us and our realtor who understands completely our model so as not to waste time with properties outside the parameters.

"Some people say we should be more diverse, but we are happy with college rental houses because our tenants will always be there as long as the college is. We have no issues with migration or population changes. All of our properties now are within three blocks of a college and are highly desirable for the tenants we market to.

"That is why real estate is a good marketing choice for me, even in a soft market. When I do my homework and believe it is a good investment given current rental prices, then I am going to go ahead with the deal.

"People who use a firm strategy in purchasing will always find opportunities to take advantage of market forces and pricing. Value investing is critical. If tenants are adequate and vacancies are limited, this investment allows for margin to be used in a way that will lend itself to mandatory repayment and positive net cash flow — unlike many strategies in the market system."

Finding good tenants is also a part of Steve's plan. He knows how important it is to market and brand your company name in the community. People want to rent from a reputable landlord. Creating a logo and quality brochures and flyers will give prospective tenants a good impression.

What is the best advice that Steve can give to anyone going into rental property investing?

"Treat your current tenants like gold. They are paying off your margin and giving you positive cash flow. They talk, so make sure they say good things about you."

Steve Aleff
V.P. Finance & Operations
218.393.2747 - cell
saleff@allovermedia.com

INVESTMENT INSIGHTS

When purchasing a home for investment purposes, you need to look at the numbers and trust your instincts. Here are a few things you can do to make the process easier:

1. Compare, compare, compare. When you think you have found the right property, inspect it again. Compare it to others you have seen and determine whether it has the features that are important to you.

2. Know the property values in the area, the growth rate, the expected growth rate, the expected income of the property, and any other information that will help you decide whether the area is good for you.

3. Do not spend much time at a property until you have crunched the numbers. You do not want to get emotionally attached to a property that makes no financial sense.

4. Do not go it alone. Ask other investors for their opinions. Ask questions and get answers from real estate agents, loan officers, and others in the business.

5. Know what you want before you get started. Determine how many investment properties you want to buy, the approximate ROI you expect from these properties, the debt level you are comfortable with, the area of town you wish to purchase in, and other similar items. Knowing what you want will keep you from wasting your time looking at homes that do not meet your needs.

6. Land will always appreciate in value. Buildings can be maintained but do not appreciate. Therefore, make sure that the value of the land is 30 percent or more of the price of the property.

7. Lowball your offers. The lower you can buy a home for below market value, the more you will make on it now and in the future. Even if the low offer is rejected, keep it on the table. They may decide to come back to it if the home stays on the market too long.

8. Get known. The more people who know you as an investment buyer, the more deals will come your way. You should get to know CPAs, lawyers, real estate agents, loan officers, and anyone else who knows about real estate investing.

Been There, Done That

Dawn Cook loves to talk of a deal that made sense no matter which way you measure it:

"We bought a commercial building that had a one bedroom apartment above it with space below for commercial use. We used the space below for our own business for a while and used the rent from the apartment above to offset our overhead. Then we rented the lower space out and the rent for that space covered our mortgage payment so the upper unit was pure profit. We later flipped it and made a nice profit."

When you have an investment property that meets your specifications, it is time to purchase it. The loan process for real estate investments is a bit different from that of a homeowner. In Chapter 6, we will review the different types of loans available to investors.

6

POT OF GOLD

You have found the perfect property, and now you want the perfect loan. You are likely to find that getting an investment loan is a bit tougher than getting a loan on your own home.

WHAT RAINBOW TO SEEK UNDER

Not all real estate loans are the same. It will be up to you to choose a loan that works for you.

There are three main loan attributes that will affect the loan and your loan payments:

1. Interest rate

2. Amortization period

3. Loan amount

A change in any one of these three can make a substantial difference to whether a property will make money.

Interest Rate

The interest rate is the amount of money you will be charged to borrow the funds. This amount is over and above the principal due. For instance, if you take out a loan for $150,000 at 7 percent interest over 30 years, the total amount of interest you will pay over the life of the loan is $209,263.35. This amount is over and above the initial loan amount of $150,000.

Interest rates differ widely from month to month and from loan to loan, which is why you must look at many different loans to find the right fit for you.

When determining how much interest will affect you, you must look at the amount borrowed and over what time. Small loans, such as a loan for $100,000, will not be affected much by interest rate variations of 1 percent or less. But large loans (in the millions) will be affected considerably, even by 0.25 percent over the period of the loan.

Amortization Period

The amortization period is the length of time used to calculate loan payments. These payments are determined assuming the loan will be repaid over the stated period. An amortization table shows a list of payments made over the life of the loan and which part of the payment is going to interest and which part to principal.

When you have a short amortization period, your loan payments will be higher, but the overall interest you pay will be less and the time it takes to acquire equity in the home will decrease. Conversely, a longer amortization period lowers your payment but increases the amount of interest paid and the time it takes to gain equity in the home.

Loan Amount

The loan amount is the amount being borrowed. The more money you borrow, the higher your loan payment will be. Some believe that putting a large amount of money down on a property, and thus making the payments low, is the best way to create a rental investment loan. However, this is an unwise idea.

When investing, you want to leverage other people's money. By doing so, you follow the axiom:

The more money you borrow, the greater will be your return on your invested capital.

By using the bank's money instead of your own, you will generate enough income to pay the loan and make a profit. The profit will be defined as a ratio based on the initial investment. Therefore, the ROI is greater when you have less of your own money invested.

Other Factors to Consider

You will also want to look at the term of the loan, the associated fees, and any prepayment penalties.

Term: The term of the loan is the life of the loan. You can have a five-year loan term amortized over a 30-year period, meaning that the payments will be based as if you will pay over a 30-year period, but the loan ends in just five years. At the end of the term, you will either have to repay the loan in full or renegotiate the loan.

Figuring out the best term for your loan depends on the plans you have for your investment. If you are planning to hold your investment for 10 years or more, you will most likely want a loan with a term that matches the amortization period. If you took a shorter term, you would be forced to refinance when the term was up and perhaps end up with a bad rate.

Long-term property works best with long-term loans. If a better financing situation becomes available during your ownership of the property, you always have the option of refinancing the loan.

If you plan to keep the property for a year or two while you rent it and fix it up, then you might want to consider a much shorter loan term. Loans with shorter terms have lower rates, which would be to your advantage. For example, a three-year Adjustable Rate Mortgage (ARM) is 0.50 to 1 percent lower than a 30-year fixed mortgage.

Fees: Loan fees can be one of the biggest expenses to an investment property financial deal. Such fees include:

- **Application fees:** Loan application fees are paid at the time the application is made and can range up to $500, but not all lenders charge such a fee. The fee is used to pay for costs of the loan officer or broker going over the application and getting the documents together to help them determine whether they can lend you money.

- **Underwriting fees:** These fees are associated with the underwriter for processing the loan application.

- **Loan origination fees (also known as origination points):** These fees are equivalent to one point or 1 percent of the total loan amount. These fees pay for the legal documents that must be drawn up and the processing of these documents.

- **Points:** A point is equal to 1 percent of your loan amount, meaning that, if you pay two points for a loan of $100,000, you would pay an extra $2,000. Points are used to get you a lower interest rate. Each point you pay will most often lower your interest rate by a quarter of a percent. Almost every lender has discount point loan levels. They may offer options with no points, one point, two points, or even more. If you plan to keep your property for a long time, paying for points up front makes sense. If you plan to sell within five years, paying points will end up costing you money.

Investor Insight: Some lenders advertise their interest with no points while others advertise their lowest possible rate that includes points. Be sure to compare apples to apples when comparison shopping for loans.

OH, THE PAPERWORK

When you are ready to take out a loan, the lender will need a long list of documents, including:

- Loan application
- Purchase agreement
- Financial statement
- Credit references
- FICA report
- Survey and Appraisal
- Property operating statements for property currently used as a rental unit
- Income and balance statements for your business
- Income tax returns for at least the last two years
- Verification of cash required for down payment
- Leases used for current rental property
- Property taxes for rental property
- Insurance binder for rental property

There are several ways to get financing for your property that do not require the traditional 20 to 40 percent down and/or the higher interest rates.

You can consider:

- Private Mortgage Lending
- No Documentation Loans
- Commercial Loans
- Option ARMS
- Seller Financing
- Owner-Occupied Loans

Financing your investment property makes sense, as long as you do your homework and choose the right loan vehicle for your needs.

Been There, Done That

Aziz Abdur-Ra'oof learned this lesson the hard way:

"I bought a home and purchased it outright. It was definitely not the right thing to do. I tied up too much money. I will try to put 10 to 20 percent down. I can do this by finding loans with private mortgage lenders. I prefer not to go through a bank due to all the excess fees and the amount of money I have to put down."

PRIVATE MORTGAGE LENDING

Private mortgage lending, sometimes referred to as hard money lending, means that you borrow your money from an individual rather than a bank. The interest rates will be higher, but the speed and ease of the deal are excellent.

You can find people who wish to be private mortgage lenders in a variety of places because most people would love to see a 10 to 12 percent return on their money with that investment secured by real estate. Anyone from a member of your church to your neighbor may be someone who can lend you money for your investment deal.

You can also approach a mortgage broker. They often have several clients who wish to invest their money this way.

A private mortgage loan does not exceed 75 percent of the loan-to-value ratio (the loan amount divided by the fair market price of the home). Let those who are potential lenders know this information and understand that the loans are done on a per property basis. In return, you will ask that they make a quick decision and can have the money to you in 10 days or less.

After your lender has approved the investment, the funds are sent to the closing attorney and held in escrow, which should make your lender feel better, too. You will never handle their money.

After the closing, your lender will receive a promissory note, a mortgage on the property, lenders' title insurance, and will be listed as the lender on the hazard insurance policy.

The process is a win-win for everyone. You only pay interest on the loan, you get no origination or discount fees, and you do not have to worry about lenders and their rules concerning investment properties. Your lender receives considerable interest and a secure investment.

It is a perfect situation if you can get the property below value.

Let us say that you can get a $100,000 property for $75,000 because it is in distress. But you have calculated that with $5,000, you can get the property up to par and then rent it out for $1,000 per month.

You find a private lender who is willing to pay the entire $75,000 at 10 percent on the property because it is only 75 percent LTV. You use $5,000 you would have spent toward a down payment to fix the property and get it rented. At the end of a year, you have paid $7,500 in interest fees and $5,000 in initial repairs while earning $12,000 in rent. This situation leaves you $500 out of pocket for the year, which is far less than a down payment of 30 percent on a loan of $75,000.

In year two, you make another $2,000 in repairs, pay another $7,500 in interest, and once again, make $12,000 in rent. This situation gives you a profit of $2,500. You do the same thing for three more years, making a total of $9,500 in profit, and then put the house up for sale. It sells for the market value of $100,000; you pay off your private lender and walk away with $25,000.

In just five years, you took $500 (your net expense at the end of year one) and turned it into nearly $35,000. You are happy and so is your lender who got their initial investment back plus $7,500 a year for five years.

You can repeat this process, even having several private loans for several different properties at once.

CASE STUDY: ETHAN DOZEMAN

Ethan Dozeman is a real estate agent, but he plans to be a real estate mogul before he is through. "I have seven properties now. My wife and I bought our first home in Grand Rapids. It was a starter house in a transitional neighborhood. We decided to move and rent it out. The renter has been there for four years. That got us started on our venture.

"My target goal is 30 by the age of 30. If I get 4 or 5 a year, I will have 30 by 30. That may be a bit aggressive, and I am willing to tone it down a bit. But I do not think there is a number of investment properties that is too many. You just have to remember that you will need to hire out more of the work and figure that into your numbers."

Ethan is realizing his dream by leveraging other people's money. Private mortgage investing has gotten him into several deals with no money down. He has also used traditional financing, but he knows that after he reaches 10 properties, he will have to get commercial loans.

"I like repossessions. I did one deal with a group of investors. They bought the house for $65,000 and signed me onto the deed. After they fixed it up, the appraised value was $106,000. I did a refinance on the property and got an 80 percent LTV, meaning I got a loan of $84,800, paid the investor back his $65,000 and another $24,000, and now have a home that is worth $106,000 with no money invested."

According to Ethan, real estate is a good investment because you have the advantage of leverage. You can go to the bank and they will loan you money on the house. You cannot get money loaned to you on the stock market. Additionally, he suggests looking at the historical ROI of real estate and the tax advantages.

CASE STUDY: ETHAN DOZEMAN

Ethan wants all of his houses close together — within a mile of each other. He wants the roof and furnace to be good and for the house to have a maintenance-free exterior. He will only pay 80 percent LTV.

Even with such restrictions, Ethan is not having any problems finding investment properties. The soft market has been advantageous to him. "I wish I had more money to buy right now due to the incredible deals. They are back to 2000 to 2001 deals. There are always deals out there. If the deal is good, then go for it. It is just a matter of finding them."

He also is not worried about earning a profit from his homes right now. "My properties are breaking even. If I can buy a property for $80,000 and it rents for $800, I can break even. It is a retirement plan. I figure that 30 homes at $1,000 a month is $30,000 a month minus repairs, vacancies, taxes, and other expenses. That will leave me with a $10,000 to $15,000 positive cash flow. At that point, I will own the homes outright."

His best experience was owning a house at 947 Ballard and finding out that the owner of 943 Ballard had lost her house to the bank. "I got it — right next to the one I have and I got it for less than the one I bought first five years ago."

Ethan learned of the sale from someone who knew he invested in homes. That is why Ethan's motto is "It is not who you know, but who knows you."

Ethan Dozeman, GRI
Associate Broker
Platinum Realty Group
(O) 616-301-6766
(C) 616-292-7329
www.DreamHomeDozeman.com

NO DOCUMENTATION LOANS

Another type of loan to consider is the No Documentation (no doc) Loan. It helps borrowers get a loan for their investments when their income, employment, or assets are difficult to prove.

There are three types of no doc loans. One is straightforward and requires no employment, income, or assets to be stated on the application. The bank simply looks at your credit profile and the value of your property.

Many no doc lenders will require just 20 percent down, as long as your credit is good. No doc loans have a bit higher interest rate, often 1 to 1½ percent higher, but if you cannot prove your income due to self-employment, or all your income comes from sources other than employment, this option may be the way to go.

Investor Insight: It is imperative that you have good credit to get started so that you can get the best deals out there.

Another type of no doc loan is the No Ratio Loan. This type of loan does not require income information, but you will need to list employment and assets. This loan will allow the lender to give you a bit lower interest rate than on the true no doc loan.

Finally, there is the Stated Income Mortgage Loan. In this type of loan, your employment and assets are verified, but your income is only stated and not verified. The lender will expect the income to be reasonable in light of your employment. Rates for this type of loan are most often 0.50 percent above a traditional loan.

OPTION ARMS

An Option ARM is an adjustable rate mortgage where the interest rate adjusts monthly and the type of payment you wish to make adjusts yearly. An Option ARM gives you control over the payment you will make, which can be good for certain cash flow needs.

There are three different payment options available with an Option ARM:

1. **Minimum Payment:** A payment schedule is set for 12 months for the least amount you can pay into the loan. It is calculated at

the interest rate in the first month. This amount cannot increase more than 7.5 percent per year.

2. **Interest Only Payment:** You do not pay principal during this period. This option is not available if the interest due is less than the minimum payment.

3. **Fully Amortizing Payment Option:** You make a typical payment based on either a 30-year or 15-year payment schedule.

Option ARMs do have prepayment penalties that are added to your loan balance when you pay off in full or if you reduce your loan by 20 percent or more in one year. This prepayment penalty holds true when you refinance the loan and if you sell the property. This penalty is most often 3 percent of your loan balance.

SELLER FINANCING

When a seller helps to finance a real estate transaction by providing finances to the buyer, it is called seller financing. A seller can take a second note on the property or finance the entire purchase price.

Seller financing is different than traditional lending because the seller will not give you cash to complete your purchase. Instead, the seller extends a credit against the purchase of his home and you execute a promissory note to them.

The interest that will be charged by an owner is negotiable. Most owner financed loans do not cost as much as traditional loans because there are no point fees. However, an owner-financer will charge you enough interest for them to earn as much as or more than they would if they were investing in Treasury Bills or CDs.

87

Seller financing offers tax breaks for sellers and alternative financing for buyers who cannot qualify for conventional loans. So, if the seller does not need the cash from the sale to buy another home, they might be willing to take the tax break and interest on the money instead.

Not every home you find will have the option of owner financing. Sellers who make good candidates for owner financing are those who own their homes free and clear — they have no mortgage.

If you are looking for an owner financed home, you will want to look at homes that are advertised that way. You will also want to look at homes listed as having little or no mortgage and then approach the owner with the idea.

You should also check into vacant and fixer-upper houses. Many people with these types of homes are ready to get out of the homeowning business. They would be happy for you to give them some money down and then make payments monthly. It is far better than having a vacant home or a home in disrepair.

If you decide to try owner financing, you will want to keep a few things in mind, such as:

- Do your research before making an offer. Just because an owner is willing to finance does not mean that the house is a good deal for you. Find comp houses in the area and crunch the numbers; only then should you make an offer.

- Be prepared to give the seller your credit report.

- The transaction time of an owner financed loan is fast since there is no formal loan process.

- Owner financing will save you money since you will have no origination fees or points.

OWNER-OCCUPIED LOANS

Most traditional home loans are owner-occupied loans, meaning that you will be occupying the property after the loan is approved. Owner-occupied loans have a more favorable loan rate than those obtained for investment purposes. However, you can get an owner-occupied loan and use it for investment — simply live there for one year.

When you take out a home loan, the lender has you sign the occupancy affidavit stating that you plan to live in the home for at least one year. If you can live in the home for a year before renting it out, then you would qualify for one of these traditional loans.

Another way to get an owner-occupied home is if you have a property with more than one unit and you plan to live in one of them. Though not a guarantee, many banks will consider you for the traditional home loan instead of an investment loan.

HOME EQUITY LOAN AND HOME EQUITY LINE OF CREDIT

A home equity loan is a loan against the equity in your home. You can get a loan of up to 100 percent of your equity, but that costs more in interest and you must have good credit. A major advantage of the home equity loan is that your interest costs can be tax deductible.

A home equity line of credit (HELOC) is similar to a home equity loan, except instead of a loan in hand, it is an open loan that can be used as you need it. The interest rate of a HELOC is tied to the Prime Rate. You only pay interest for the amount of money you use, and the interest can be written off as a tax deduction. A HELOC is a good choice if you want to have money available, but do not know exactly when you may need it or how much you may need.

Since you plan to buy investment property, you may as well use the equity in the home you already have. It also makes sense to use that money to make the right purchase, even if you have to take a little longer to shop for the right loan later on.

Been There, Done That

Debbie Malone used a second mortgage to get her first investment property.

"When we bought our first investment, it was with a second mortgage. Now we use a line of credit. It enables us to put a lower cash offer on a property and close in days. This works well when you have a seller who needs to close quickly. If we are flipping the property, we renovate as quickly as possible to sell fast and pay off the line of credit. If we decide to keep it, we get a mortgage on the property, pay off the line of credit, and look for the next property."

REFINANCING AN INVESTMENT PROPERTY

When you have a loan, do not put it all away and never think about it again until you sell. Always be on the lookout for better loan offers and constantly consider whether refinancing your property makes good financial sense.

One reason you may want to consider refinancing is to increase your cash flow. If you have built up equity in the property, you could use that equity instead of having it tied up. If you refinance to a lower rate or increase the term, your monthly expenses could also go down.

You can then use the equity to make improvements to your property, such as putting on a new roof, upgrading kitchens and baths, buying new appliances, or re-siding the house. You can also use the money to invest in more properties.

The major benefit of real estate investing is the ability to benefit from the equity in the property. If you have it, you may as well use it to increase your investment holdings.

After you have your loan, it is time to prepare the home to rent. In Chapter 7, we will explore the types of maintenance and repairs to expect and how to make repairs if you already have a tenant in place.

7

TIP TOP SHAPE

As a landlord today, you will need to keep your investment in pristine order; you will also want to make improvements. Doing so will make a big difference in the profitability of the property.

You may need to replace windows or doors, add a new roof, replace appliances, replace or add siding, or complete a host of other projects. Although doing so costs some money, it will eventually generate big profits by allowing you to charge more rent and by causing the property to appreciate.

First, you must prepare a property for habitation. The property must be safe for renters. Cosmetic repairs, such as new paint, should be taken care of. Floors, fixtures, appliances, and windows should be clean. The exterior should be presentable. Garbage needs to be disposed of properly.

Maintaining a property includes repairing units after old tenants leave and fixing problems while the unit is currently rented.

Finally, maintaining a property means adding those little extras that give your property more worth.

READY OR NOT, HERE THEY COME

As soon as you purchase your first rental home, you become a landlord, even if you have no tenants. You have to immediately think like a landlord and determine what needs to be done to your home to make it ready for your first tenant.

Let There Be Light

Even if no one is in the home, you will need to have the utilities on. You will need electricity and water to do all the cleaning and repairing. During the winter months, you will want the home to have electricity to keep the pipes from freezing. After the cleaning and repairing are finished, you will need the utilities on to show the home.

Investor Insight: If you live in a cold area, have a plumber or electrician install heat tape on the water pipes in your investment home. When the temperature in the area where the pipes are located drops below a specified temperature, the tape, plugged into the electricity, will turn on and heat the pipes until the area surrounding the pipes has heated sufficiently to keep them from freezing.

Even if a tenant vacates the property, you need to be sure to keep the electricity and water turned on. Many utility companies offer a service to landlords allowing them to keep continual service, called leave-on service.

With leave-on service, the utility company knows that when a tenant calls to cancel the service, it should be taken out of their name and put back into yours. Although this service does cost money for the switch, it does not cost as much as reconnecting each time and it gives you peace of mind that the property will not be without electricity without your knowledge.

When you have the electricity in your name, you will want to turn off the breaker to the electric water heater to lower your bills when you are not using hot water for cleaning.

Prepare to Prepare

Your unit may have remnants from the last owner or the last tenant. It will be up to you to get rid of the bed frame they did not take or the old sofa in the garage.

> **Investor Insight:** Know the laws in your area. Some states or local governments have passed laws concerning how long a landlord must hold onto items before they can legally dispose of them.

After you have gotten rid of the items left over, it is time to make a list of things to do.

Walk through each room, including the garage and basement, and write down what you see and anything you think needs to be done. Do the same with the exterior and yard of the home.

Make It Shine

Your property is the product that your business is selling. As a landlord, the "sale" is either by month or by year, but you want to attract a "buyer" who will keep your property in good condition. You can attract the right kind of tenant, and charge top dollar for your property, if it is well taken care of. Cleanliness is key.

To save yourself time and money, take all your cleaning items with you. The time you save from having to go back and forth, and the money you will save by not buying items at a more expensive convenience store, will be worth the effort to get your cleaning kit together before leaving home.

Here is a good list of cleaning items:

- Vacuum cleaner
- Broom
- Dustpan
- Mop and bucket
- Rags and sponges
- Cleaners and disinfectants
- Air freshener
- Toilet bowl brush
- Rubber gloves
- Trash bags
- Smoke alarm batteries
- Light bulbs
- Sandpaper
- Touch up paint
- Patching compound for nail holes
- Hammer, screwdrivers, pliers, and other typical tools

Some cleaning is obvious — take out the trash, sweep and mop the floor, and vacuum the carpeting — but your tenants want and deserve more than that. They expect you to do such things as:

- Clean the walls of your unit to remove fingerprints and marks. If you allowed smoking in the home, you will also need to wipe down ceilings to get rid of tobacco smoke stain and the smell that goes with it.

- Clean appliances thoroughly, cleaning the grease and mildew off of refrigerators and stoves, cleaning the microwave, running the dishwasher to be sure that the inside is clean, and cleaning the oven.

- Clean kitchen and bathroom sinks and countertops, toilets, and tubs.

- Use bleach on discolored porcelain.

- Clean and shine all windows and storm windows.

- Clean garbage disposal and run a lemon through it to get rid of odors.

- Change air filters for the air conditioning and heating units.

Investor Insight: Have your unit ready before showing it to potential renters. Applicants will notice the dirty floor or walls and will not want to rent — even if you tell them what you plan to do before they move in.

You may decide that hiring a cleaning agency is worth the price because they can get it done right and fast. You may have to spend two days cleaning the house, and a good team from an agency can get it done in an afternoon. That kind of time savings can be used to start looking for a good tenant.

Looking Down

Carpeting is one area that you need to focus on. Check to see if it is spotted, worn, or outdated in style or color. You would not want to try to rent a house with gold shag carpet from the late '70s.

If you buy new carpet, look for something traditional in style and color. A small nap, tan carpet is a good choice. The short nap will help the carpet last longer, and the color will go with just about anything your renter owns in terms of furniture or décor.

If you have more than one unit, you will want to eventually have the same carpet in each unit. This strategy will help you out if you need a carpet remnant and will also keep the decision making process easy.

If the carpeting is in good shape, you will want to steam clean it after spot cleaning any major stains, making the carpet look good and smell fresh. The goal is to get the unit rented as quickly as possible, and clean floors will help you do that.

Pesky Pests

Pest control is part of the clean up process before renting to a new tenant. The best way to keep pests at bay is to exclude them in the first place.

- Seal cracks where pests can enter the home.

- Place insecticide, on a regular basis, around the foundation and soil around the foundation.

- Use a residual insecticide in the house along the baseboards and windows.

- Use baits to get rid of ants.

- Keep gutters and downspouts cleaned out.

- Slope soil away from foundation to keep excess water from pooling.

- Keep trees and shrubs trimmed.

It may be in your best interest to hire a pest control company to eliminate pests and then make monthly or quarterly visits to the property to keep pests at bay. To find a good pest control company, you can look in the yellow pages. Be sure that they, and their technicians, are licensed. Also find out what pesticides they will use and ask for the least toxic one available.

Your tenant has the right to know about the pesticide treatments. They need to be given a notice before application. Check with state laws to determine how much notice is required in your area.

Been There, Done That

Dawn Cook relates her own pest escapade:

"We once had raccoons in the attic space of our commercial apartment and those creatures are hard to get rid of. We hired a trapper to catch them and he had to take them 70 miles away to release them. Apparently they can find their way back if you release them too close to the area that you removed them from."

Paint It Pretty

Sometimes, no amount of washing will get rid of the stains or the dingy look of dirt. Painting the walls and ceilings of a home, and any exterior wood, can make a home feel brand new.

If painting outside, be sure to use exterior grade paint. Keeping outside wood painted looks good, protects the wood, and makes the wood last longer. Consider using light trim on a darker colored home to make your home appear larger.

You may find that it is necessary to paint the exterior of the home or perhaps add new siding. The decision is yours to make, but do not assume that siding is significantly more expensive. Check the price of both and take into account that you will not need to do anything to the siding other than pressure wash it yearly, whereas you will need to repaint every five to 10 years.

A good tip when painting your rental unit is to consider a color scheme and then stick with it throughout the exterior and all the rooms. If you have more than one rental unit, stick with the same theme throughout each unit as well. This tip will save you time and money with touch up paint.

Investor Insight: The only time this strategy does not work is if you have two units side by side. In this case, you will not want them to have identical exterior colors, but you can have the interiors the same.

Down Below

Your basement is often where you will find the heating systems, water heaters, electrical panel boxes, and water pipes. You may also have a gas meter, oil tank meter, or sewer line in the basement. All of these must be checked and maintained on a regular basis.

You will also want to be sure that the basement staircase railings and steps are secure and sturdy.

Safe and Sound

Safety is paramount where your tenants are concerned. If something happens to a tenant and it is due to something that was in disrepair or not up to code, you will be liable for their medical bills and can be sued civilly for damages.

Here are some things you should do when considering the safety of your tenants:

- Make sure faulted outlets next to sinks are grounded.

- Provide proper bathroom ventilation to prevent mold.

- Keep all smoke detectors in good working condition. Be sure to check your local laws to determine the number of detectors needed and the proper placement of these detectors.

- Make sure all doors have working handles.

- Make sure that windows can be opened and have working locks.

- Provide a fire extinguisher for the kitchen and check it every time you enter the home to be sure it is fully charged.

- Install a carbon monoxide detector if there is a fireplace or wood heater in the home.

- Tack down loose carpeting.

- Take care of exposed wiring.

- Let your tenants know what you would expect them to do in case of a fire.

- Replace door locks after each tenant leaves.

- Have the area around the home well lit at night.

- Abide by all local health and safety codes.

If you have a multi-tenant unit, you will also need to keep common areas clean and safe at all times.

Curb Appeal

Many building owners think about just that — the building. However, you own the entire package, which includes the building and the property surrounding it. Having the property look good will help you maintain high rents, attract good tenants, and raise the value of your property.

You will need to mow the lawn and trim the bushes. Caring for your property presents you as a responsible landlord and attracts good tenants who will help you keep the rent checks coming in.

CASE STUDY: NEAL BLOOME

Neal Bloome is a realtor and a real estate investor in Florida. He is a hands-on landlord, along with his partner, who collects the rent, keeps the books, and pays the bills. He has subcontractors on his team who can handle repairs and maintenance.

As he gets ready to put one of his properties on the rental market, he makes sure that the unit is clean and that all appliances and services are in working order. Neal works mostly with Section 8 housing, which has some pretty strict rules.

"Section 8 housing, in a nut shell, is guaranteed rent from the government. It is for people who do not make enough income to live and pay rent. How they qualify will determine how much of the rent will be paid for them, but most is covered. In order for the government to be willing to subsidize the rents, they want to be sure that the apartments meet their standards."

If you wish to have your unit Section 8 approved, you will have to have it inspected. The inspector will examine the interior and exterior of the building, the plumbing and heating, the exits, each room, and all common areas to see if they are in good condition. The inspection must be made when the unit is vacant. All the utilities must be turned on and the inspector has to have access to the common areas.

The inspectors are trained to look for specific things found on the HUD form (see Appendix). For each item on the form, the inspector will mark pass or fail. If repairs are needed, that is noted on the form as well.

"For us, Section 8 housing has been both good and bad. It is good because you are assured of the rent each month, as long as the tenant remains in compliance with Section 8 laws. It is bad because we have seen more damage in our Section 8 rental units than in those that are not Section 8. Even with the damage, though, we have found this to be a good way to meet our financial goals."

CASE STUDY: NEAL BLOOME

When not using Section 8 as a source for tenants, Neal and his partner find and keep tenants the old fashioned way. When asked how he keeps a good tenant, Neal replied, "You need to be proactive to their needs and keep their rents reasonable. If you do these two things, keeping a good tenant is easy."

Neal Bloome
ReMax Hometown Inc.
2500 Weston Road #103
Weston FL 33331
954-608-5556 Direct
954-212-0257 Fax

REPAIR WHILE THEY ARE THERE

Every investor of real estate needs to understand the benefit of repairing something as quickly as possible. Imagine a loose toilet. If taken care of immediately, it takes simply tightening a bolt. If you wait a bit longer, you will have to replace the wax seal at the base of the toilet. Wait even longer and you will have to replace the flooring around the toilet due to leakage. You may even have to replace the toilet if it breaks near the base. If the toilet is located in an upstairs bathroom, you will eventually have to repair the ceiling below. The damage just gets worse.

If the cost and extent of damage is not enough to convince you, consider your tenants. The goal of your investment business is to make money, and the only way you can make money is by receiving rent. If you do not take care of damages, you will lose tenants and be left with a repair bill.

Most state and local laws require that you maintain a rental property to a certain standard. Such standards include adequate shelter from the elements, heat, water, electricity, cleanliness, and sound structure. You will also be in charge of keeping your property up-to-date on local housing codes for light, ventilation, and wiring.

Investor Insight: You can find out about local laws by going to your local housing authority or fire department. Be sure you know the code so that you are not penalized for violations.

If you do not fix items that need to be fixed in a timely manner, your tenant has several different courses of action to possibly take. For instance, he can withhold the rent, hire someone to make the repairs and take that off his rent, call the building inspector who will order you to make the repair, or even move out despite having a lease. Worst of all, he could sue you for discomfort, annoyance, and emotional distress. Even if he did not win, the cost of the lawyer and the time spent in court could have been used elsewhere.

To make repairs on a unit, you have to have the tenant's permission to enter. Permission is not a problem when a tenant has contacted you with a repair issue, but there are times when you may want to make a repair they have not requested or when you want to make an inspection.

To enter the premises, you most often have to give a 24 hour advanced notice. (See Appendix for the law of your state regarding landlord entry.) The only time this notice is not required is in cases of emergency.

Emergencies include:

- Frozen pipes
- Water leak
- Suspected gas leak
- Fire
- Broken window, door, or lock

The best thing you can do is to handle the repair as soon as possible or have someone handle it for you. The rule of thumb is that major repairs like heating or plumbing should be addressed within 24 hours and minor repairs within 48 hours.

JUST A LITTLE EXTRA

Round and Round

Ceiling fans in a room will make a good first impression on your tenants. They will also add light and help reduce heating and cooling bills. Ceiling fans cool the air by about seven degrees. If you use the fans in reverse during the winter, it can bring the warm air from the furnace that rises to the ceiling back down to floor level, making you feel warmer without have to turn up the heat.

Choose the right size ceiling fan for the room, then install it 12 inches from the ceiling to allow the air to circulate.

42 inches	up to 100 ft.²
52 inches	100 to 400 ft.²
56 inches	more than 400 ft.²

Open and Close

Another way to spruce up a rental unit is to add mini-blinds to the windows. Mini-blinds look good and help conserve energy. If you have the blinds pulled against the sun in the summer, your cooling bills will decrease. If you have them open to the sun in the winter, your heating bills decrease. Having them in your unit sounds good when written in your classified ad.

Mini-blinds are inexpensive, can be bought at any local department store, and are easy to install. Have your window measurements with you when you go to shop for them. The best color for a rental unit is something neutral like cream or white.

Shutters

A good way to add spice to a building with little cost and no maintenance is by adding a set of shutters. If you purchase the plastic kind, you can install them with just six screws in 10 minutes.

Shutters make a home appear larger, better kept, and even more expensive. They do not need to be placed on the back windows, but any windows on the front or windows seen from the road should have them.

White or cream shutters are best. They go with any color you have chosen for the outside your home. If you have a white home, you may want to consider black shutters instead.

Say It with Flowers

Adding a few simple flowers or plants to the exterior of your home can make it feel more welcoming. Put the flowers in the flowerbed or a pretty outdoor planter.

You do not have to know much about plants to make your home more appealing. You also do not need to spend much money. The good thing about adding plants is that your tenants will take care of them after they move in, and the exterior of the home will continue to look beautiful and inviting.

Investor Insight: Be sure that you remove dead flowers during the winter months. A clean but empty flower bed is far more appealing than one full of brown, dead weeds and flowers.

Give Your Kitchen and Bath a Facelift

When a home is for sale, kitchens and baths are a big selling point. The same is true when tenants are looking for a place to rent. Here are some inexpensive things you can do to these two rooms that will increase the value of your home in the future and allow you to gain more income now:

- Change the doorknobs or handles.

- Paint stained cabinets white.

- Put down new laminate flooring.

- Install lighting under the cabinets.

- Give the rooms a fresh coat of paint.

- Add a kitchen island for more counter and storage space.

- Update sinks to white or stainless if they have an outdated color such as harvest gold or avocado green.

Having a kitchen and baths that look fresh and up-to-date will help you rent your unit faster and for more money.

Go Green

Everyone wants to save money, including your tenants. If you do things to make your rental unit more energy efficient, you will attract more tenants and you will increase the value of the property when you are ready to sell.

- Be sure the home is well insulated.

- Have the HVAC equipment checked regularly — systems that work properly are more energy efficient.

- When you purchase new appliances, purchase the energy-efficient variety.

- Insulate the doors and windows.

If you call your local electric company, they can provide you with pamphlets explaining what you can do to create an energy efficient home. Although not all the techniques are something that you can do as a landlord — it is not up to you to turn off the lights as your tenant leaves the room — you can learn about energy saving appliances and proper insulation.

In many areas, utility companies, nonprofits, or government agencies will help landlords create an energy efficient rental property through subsidies, tax breaks, and even grants.

When you have found the right rental home, gotten it financed in a way that meets your financial goals, and have it clean, repaired, and ready to rent, it is time for a tenant. Chapter 8 will reveal how to find a good tenant.

YOU ARE THE ONE
THAT I NEED

If your rental property business is to be successful, you will have to maintain good landlord-tenant relationships. Finding and then keeping tenants will be your goal. This chapter will reveal how to successfully advertise for tenants and then screen them to see if the relationship will be a good fit.

MAKE NEW FRIENDS, BUT KEEP THE OLD

Finding good tenants is essential, but keeping the old ones will help you maintain a property with few vacancy bumps along the way.

When you buy a property, especially a multi-tenant property, you may "inherit" some old tenants. As long as there is nothing on their record to indicate that they make poor tenants, your goal should be to keep them.

Do tenants "transfer" with the property when you purchase the property? That depends.

If the tenants have a lease, then you purchase their leases with the property and have to honor that agreement. If the tenants do not have a lease or are leased on a month-to-month basis, then it will be up to you to keep the tenants or allow them to leave.

Investor Insight: When you inherit tenants, you also inherit any deposits they paid and you will have to honor the return policy on those deposits.

Having a tenant transfer to a new landlord does not have to be difficult. For each old tenant who moves, you incur an expense and so do they. Keeping them in their current place of residence is a win-win situation for both you and them.

Moving is not just inconvenient; it is also expensive (and not just for the vacating tenant). Move-outs create landlord expenses, too. According to experts, bringing in a new customer can cost six times as much as keeping an old one — thus their gold status.

Determine what drew your tenants to the property in the first place:

- Amenities?

- Good service?

- Rent prices?

Understanding what your current tenants want and figuring out how to provide it for them is the key to keeping them.

STOP AND LOOK

If you are purchasing a property with no tenants or you have vacancies to fill, a good way to let people know is to place yard signs on the property.

Yard signs are simple and inexpensive. They are also incredibly effective. Many of your potential tenants will come from the surrounding area.

Either they already live in the area and are looking for a new home or they live in the area and have a friend looking to find a place in the same neighborhood. It is even possible that someone just driving by on their way to somewhere else happens to see your sign.

The little signs from the hardware store can be used, but using a more professional sign will get you higher-end applicants. Consider purchasing the kind of sign that a realtor would use, with a solid frame that will hold up in the wind and will not deteriorate in the rain.

Your sign should have the words "For Rent" and your phone number. You may also put a Web site domain where you can have photos of the interior of the house or unit and a description of the amenities of the property.

You may also want to put out directional signs. These are signs at the end of the road that point to your rental. You have seen these types of signs used by real estate agencies and even yard sales.

Professionals and amateurs alike use signs because they work. As you try to find new tenants, make signs a top priority.

> **Investor Insight:** Yard signs are especially effective if you live in a college town and will be renting to college students.

PUT IT IN PRINT

In addition to signs, newspaper advertisements in the classified section are also a traditional way to attract new tenants. When looking for a place to rent, many start by looking in the classified section of the newspaper. Potential tenants who are out of town can log onto the online version of the paper and search as well.

Investor Insight: Consider your target audience. If your typical tenant is a college student, for instance, then you might want to consider posting your ad with the campus paper, but be aware of the Fair Housing Act detailed below. If you post on campus, be sure to post in other locations as well.

Your ad should describe the benefits of your property and should contain an address, a price, deposit information, availability, and contact information. If you are not comfortable providing a complete address, provide a subdivision name or the section of town. Doing so will help limit calls to those who wish to rent in that area. Here are a few examples to get you started:

SAMPLE AD EXAMPLES

2BR/1.5BA RENOVATED rustic home in Pinebluff. 1,300 square feet. New kitchen, bath, & wood floors. $700/month. $700 deposit. Application & lease required. Available June 1st. 555-555-1234.

3BR/1.75BA brick home in Eagle Springs. Safe neighborhood with large yard. $550/month. $550 deposit. Available immediately. Call 555-555-1234.

3BR/2BA Brick home w/central heat and AC, hardwood and tile floors, gas logs and garage. Convenient to SP & PH. Located off Morganton Rd. $1,100 deposit and per mo. Call Bob at 555-555-1234.

DETAILED AD EXAMPLE

This extraordinary condo has 1 bedroom, 1 bathroom, large living room, large kitchen, and a private veranda. Appliances include stove, refrigerator, dishwasher, microwave, A/C, electric heat, and a washer/dryer. Reserved underground parking space. Bicycle storage in garage. Close to Whole Foods, Harris Teeter, the Riler Park Bike Path, and the Riler Mall. No pets. $1,500/ month and deposit. Available July 15. To learn more, call 555-555-1234.

Research Triangle Park condo. Easy access to downtown, transit, and the Capitol. In walking distance from the Center Street Mall and local downtown restaurants. Quiet community. Exercise facility. Come see this beautiful condo!!!! $1,450/month plus deposit. Available immediately. To learn more, please call 555-555-1234.

Your goal is to find tenants who are willing and able to make their rent payments in full and on time each month. You want someone who is likely to keep your unit clean and in good condition. You want someone who will follow your policies, but you need to be careful how you word your ads so they are not discriminatory.

Federal laws prevent landlords from seeking out particular groups of people or disregarding others.

- **The Civil Rights Act** — You cannot discriminate against someone based on race.

- **Fair Housing Act** — You cannot discriminate based on race, color, sex, national origin, family status, disabilities, or religion.

Most states, and even many local governments, have their own laws concerning discrimination and housing that go beyond the federal standards. In addition to those items listed in the Fair Housing Act, a locality may add occupation, sexual orientation, or citizenship status.

The Fair Housing Act has two specific provisions concerning the advertising of rental properties:

1. You may not make statements, written or oral, or even in pictures, that would indicate that you would rather have one type of tenant over another. You may not even imply a preferred number of children.

2. You have to post your ad either in a widely-read newspaper or on widely-read bulletin boards. You may not post your ad for limited group viewing only. If you wish to post to a specific, limited audience publication, be sure to post your ad in additional, more diverse publications as well.

Phrases to avoid include:

- Adult couple
- No children
- Spanish speaking
- Male only
- Close to XYZ Church

How do pictures enter into the mix? If you show a photo of your apartment complex, for instance, with people at the pool and the mix of people in terms of race are not indicative of the race of the population in the area, you can be sued for discrimination. Someone can suggest that by showing 60 percent Asian tenants in the photo, you are stating in pictures that you prefer to rent to Asian people.

If you show a photo during the holidays that has a Christmas tree, you can find yourself in similar trouble. You can be accused of discriminating against any religion that does not celebrate Christmas.

Here are some tips to keep advertisements in compliance with the laws:

1. Review your ad thoroughly before placing it. If you think there is a chance that it looks discriminatory, start again.

2. Add the Fair Housing Logo to all your printed materials.

3. Put a Fair Housing message in your advertisement (i.e., "Landlord does not discriminate on the basis of race, color, religion, national origin, sex, handicap or familial status").

4. Only describe the apartment and the amenities. You should not state who you think would be happy renting from you.

5. Only use photos of the unit itself. Then you will not have to worry about whether the people shown represent the population of your area.

6. If you are not sure, leave it out. It is better to leave out a phrase and be safe than to find out you have written an ad in violation of the Fair Housing Act.

For more on advertising and the Fair Housing Act, see this HUD bulletin: **http://www.hud.gov/offices/fheo/disabilities/sect804achtenberg.pdf.**

AGE OF TECHNOLOGY

In the age of technology, you may want to consider finding your tenants via the Internet. Posting on the Internet is inexpensive, and depending on the site you use, can be completely free.

In addition to a low cost, Internet listings have another benefit — space. With newspaper classifieds, the more you write, the more it costs. When you post online, space restrictions are removed. You will have the freedom to write as much as you think necessary.

To post on the Internet, you can create your own Web site, create a blog, or find a site that allows you to post. If you have a large number of investment properties, a property with a large number of units, or a business that already has a Web site, creating a Web site for your properties makes sense.

Duayne Weir of Investment Realties, LLC and Market Link Realty is a realtor and investor. He has two different sites. His Investment Realties site helps investors find appropriate properties, and his Market Link Realty site is a more traditional site for the buying and selling of homes.

Since Duayne already had a site for traditional buying and selling, he has added a page to find tenants who wish to rent/lease to own: **http://www.duayneweir.com/Rent_to_Own/page_1791230.html.**

Adding a page to his Web site did not cost any additional money. Since he has the capabilities to add properties easily, time was not a factor. Clicking on one of the homes he has listed will give you far more details and photos than could be seen in a traditional advertisement.

For Duayne, this method works because his Web site is viewed often by people who are looking for a place of their own. He does not have to worry about creating traffic to his site.

If you do not have the skills necessary to create your own Web site or the price of doing so is prohibitive given your investment properties, you might consider creating a blog. Going to **www.blogger.com**, you can create a site in an hour and do not need any HTML skills. You simply follow the instructions, add photos and descriptions, and give your contact information. In the end, you will have a specific Web address for potential tenants to view the property.

The problem with creating a blog is that no one will know it is there or be able to find it because it has no traffic and will not be in the search engines fast enough. Therefore, using a blog is a good way to supplement other forms of advertising. For instance, if you have a sign in the yard, you would be able to put the blog address on the sign and those interested in the property could find out more information.

Investor Insight: If you choose to have a Web site or blog, use the Web address on all of your advertising materials such as signs, other ads, and flyers.

Finally, you can find a Web site that will allow you to list your property. Some sites, such as **www.rentalhouses.com** or **www.rentmarketer.com** charge a fee for the listing. Other sites, such as **www.craigslist.org**, allow you to place your ad for free.

No matter how you choose to advertise online, there are certain elements that should be included in an online advertisement:

1. **Location:** Include the property address and list location amenities. What makes your property unique in terms of location? List all the location amenities. Rather than just say "Close to shopping centers," with an online listing you can say, "Close to XYZ and 123 Shopping Centers."

2. **Rent:** State your rent. Better yet, state your rent with the median rent for similar properties in your neighborhood.

3. **Apartment features:** Include items such as number of square feet, number of beds and baths, parking, playground, fenced yard, basement, swimming pool, deck, patio, and hot tub, as well as any others that will attract tenants.

4. **Utility cost:** Let your prospective tenant know what the average monthly bills have been for the last 12 months. You can also state which utility companies serve the area.

5. **Lease requirements:** List deposits that will be needed, including any deposit for pets. Also list lease restrictions such as non-smoking unit or need for renter's insurance.

6. **Lead Paint Disclosure**

7. **Vacancy date:** Let the reader know when the unit will be available.

Been There, Done That

Jane, an investor in Florida, had this to say about advertising.

"I paid to put my ad in a few local papers. The smaller paper seemed to get the most response. But in the end, I found my tenant from advertising on Craigslist. I try to buy homes that I would live in, so I advertised the way I would look for a place to rent. I would go to Craigslist.

"I do have a caution, however. Craigslist has scammers. People will call you with many sob stories. I had people calling to tell me about losing their job, being recently divorced, or having some other problem in order for me to waive the one thing I stated clearly in the advertisement — I would be checking their credit and past references.

"The first thing I told everyone who called was that I definitely would be checking landlord and employment history for the last two consecutive years with no exceptions. After I stated that clearly, the majority of people hung up the phone.

"I think that advertising somewhere like Craigslist is a good idea. It worked for me — I have a great renter who pays on time."

LET ME TELL YOU ABOUT...

Another good way to get tenants is through referrals. These referrals can come from friends, neighbors, and family. People who know you have a property for rent will often know of someone who is looking.

It is important, however, that you do not take referrals without checking them out as thoroughly as you would any other applicant. Your best friend may believe that John Smith would make the perfect tenant, but your best friend may not know the whole story.

If you have more than one rental unit, especially if you have an apartment complex, you might want to consider a referral program. This type of program gives your tenant a gift of some kind for every referral that results in a lease.

Such gifts can include:

- Gift cards to stores

- A prepaid credit card

- A free month's rent

- A check for a specified amount of money

Such incentives can help you find tenants similar to the ones you already have without much work on your part.

Been There, Done That

Debbie Malone had this happen to her:

"We rented to a young guy, who then recommended his mother and then his grandmother. We rented those three properties to all three family members for several years. What an easy way to get a good tenant!"

GPS OF RENTAL TENANTS

If you do not have the time to find your own tenants, you may want to consider having someone find them for you. Locator services are companies that can find tenants for any kind of residential rental unit, although some specialize in condos, townhouses, apartments, or single-family dwellings. You can find a locator service by looking in the Yellow Pages, often under the section "Real Estate Services" or "Rental Agencies."

Locator companies represent many owners and have a consolidated list of vacancies in the area. Those looking to rent a home contact the locator company and are given a list of properties that meet their specifications, such as two bedrooms or near the transit line.

The service saves the renter the hassle of looking through all the different advertisements and saves you the hassle of advertising.

The property owner, not the renter, pays the fee to the locator company. Fees are about 50 percent of a month's rent, but if the company does not find a tenant for you, you will owe nothing. Depending on the rent of your property, this service may not be a good deal for you.

> **Investor Insight:** Using a locator service is more cost effective if you use a year lease since the price is low relative to the turnover ratio of your property. On the other hand, six-month leases or month-to-month leases increase the relative cost and may make the service an unwise choice.

COME ON IN

Having an open house is a good way to get people to see what you have to offer. If you do it right, you may only have to hold one open house to find your tenant. There is one big advantage to having an open house — time.

You will be able to show your property once instead of several times. If you have 10 people come through your open house in three hours, you are showing your house much more efficiently than if you had to show your property 10 different times.

Here are some tips to make your open house successful:

1. Market the open house through classified ads, yard and directional signs, and by letting any local organizations you belong to know of the open house.

2. Have all repairs complete before the open house. It is important that prospective tenants see the property as it will be when they rent it.

3. Provide cookies or other light snacks as a way to have a potential tenant stick around long enough for you to ask questions of them in a non-threatening situation.

4. Many tenants will make a decision based on the outside of the property. Be sure to have the entrance looking clean and nice. You will want to have the yard in good condition as well.

5. Have the unit clean and free from odors. Cleanliness includes freshly cleaned carpeting, windows, and appliances.

6. Set the thermostat in the unit so that those visiting will be comfortable. If it is too hot or too cold, they may wonder if the HVAC unit is working correctly.

Been There, Done That

For Duayne Weir, one of his best landlord stories comes from getting tenants based on a recommendation from someone at his church:

"I let five intern teenage boys live in one of my two-bedroom units. These kids were the best, even though they were not paying the rent directly. They were polite, kind, and mature. They kept the place fairly clean for a bunch of pre-college young men. And they were on the road doing their ministry most of the time, so they were gone 280 days of the year."

ACCEPTING SECTION 8 TENANTS

Many landlords find tenants through the Section 8 housing program. Those who receive Section 8 get vouchers from their housing agency to help pay their rent. The federal government is in charge of the program and, therefore, in charge of the rent payment.

To accept Section 8 voucher holders, you need to contact your local Housing Authority and when you advertise, state that you accept Section 8 voucher holders. But just because you accept these holders does not mean that they have to rent your property. Just as with any tenant, they may choose where they live.

You also need to understand that you, not the government, are responsible for choosing your tenants. Just because a tenant has a Section 8 voucher does not mean that the tenant has been screened by the Housing Authority. You need to screen these applicants like you would any others.

According HUD, "Once a PHA approves an eligible family's housing unit, the family and the landlord sign a lease and, at the same time, the landlord and the PHA sign a housing assistance payments contract that runs for the same term as the lease. This means that everyone — tenant, landlord, and PHA — has obligations and responsibilities under the voucher program."

Tenants are obligated to:

- Sign a lease for one year

- Pay a security deposit if required by the landlord

- Comply with the lease

- Pay their share of the rent on time

- Keep the unit in good condition

The landlord is obligated to:

- Provide safe and sanitary housing as determined by the housing program's inspections

- Provide housing at a reasonable rent

- Provide all services agreed on in the lease

Now that you know how to bring in potential renters, you will need to know how to screen them and determine who is the right one for you. In Chapter 9, we will explore methods for qualifying your tenants.

9

MORE THAN JUST A GUESSING GAME

When it comes to choosing a tenant, you should not just play a guessing game.

To get what you want, and to be fair to those who wish to live on your property, you need to establish a selection criteria. There are three general things you want when finding a new tenant:

1. Ability to pay in a timely manner

2. Willingness to abide by the lease and all the provisions in the lease

3. No sense that illegal activity will be engaged in or on your property

PAY ON TIME, EVERY TIME

As a landlord, you are a business owner, first and foremost. To be successful, you have to have tenants who pay the rent. Without the rent, your investment is not going to bring in a profit or, for that matter, break even. You cannot afford to rent to someone who cannot pay.

Verify Income

The first thing you need to do is verify the income information provided by the applicant. This income will be in the form of a salary, social security, disability, and/or child support.

Income Ratios

After you have verified the income of your applicant, you will want to look at their income versus their expenses. This income ratio is used by lenders to determine whether someone is able to handle a mortgage payment. The Fannie Mae's Community Home Buyer's Program benchmark of 33 percent is a good measuring stick. This figure means that the rent should be 33 percent or less of the total income.

To measure this ratio, multiply the applicant's gross monthly income (income before taxes) by 0.33. If the resulting number is more than your rent, they are above the ratio.

For instance, if you have an applicant who makes $2,000 per month, you would multiply $2,000 by 0.33 to get $660. If your rent is $600, they fall in the income ratio. If your rent is $700, it slightly exceeds the ratio. If the rent is $800, the rent is far above the ratio.

Of course, a ratio is just an arbitrary number. You need to use your common sense and gut feeling as well. If the applicant has an excellent credit history and good references, having an income ratio of 40 percent may not be a problem. But if the applicant's ratio is 29 percent and they have a history of nonpayment, you may want to ignore the ratio altogether in lieu of this information.

Credit Check

You will want to check your applicant's credit history. A credit report can give you a detailed picture of your applicant's payment history to credit card companies, loan institutions, stores, doctors' offices, and other commercial enterprises. You can either get the report yourself or you can hire a tenant screening specialist.

To do it yourself, you can order a credit report, for a small fee, from the following agencies:

Equifax
PO Box 740256
Atlanta, GA 30374
800-685-1111
www.equifax.com

Experian
PO Box 2002
Allen, TX 75013
888-397-3742
www.experian.com

TransUnion LLC
PO Box 2000
Chester, PA 19022
800-888-4213
www.transunion.com

In addition to seeing the payment history of your applicant, you can also see how much debt the applicant has. To get such a report, you will need to have your applicant's social security number and a copy of the deed to your property. You will also need your applicant's written permission.

Investor Insight: Many landlords charge a fee to the applicants to cover the cost of the credit check. If you choose not to do so, keep receipts of the credit checks you run because the fees are tax deductible.

You can also check their history in a less traditional way, especially if the applicant is young and has not had the time to establish much in the way of credit. You can contact utility companies that the applicant has used in the past. If you cannot obtain this information from the company itself, ask the applicant to provide you with documentation that the bills were paid on time.

CHARACTER COUNTS

When it comes to abiding by the lease and being a law abiding citizen, you are seeking to determine the character of the applicant. Someone may pay their bills on time and have good income, but be someone who does not like to follow the rules or who has a criminal background.

To find out about an applicant's character, you will need to ask others who know him or her.

References

One of the best ways to determine if an applicant will follow the rules on the lease is by asking a previous landlord. If an applicant was willing to follow the old lease, you have an indication that they will do so for you. The same holds true for illegal activity.

When you talk to the previous landlord(s), ask the following questions:

1. Did the applicant pay on time?

2. Did they leave the unit clean and in good repair?

3. Did they give proper notice when moving?

4. Did they observe all the rental policies?

5. Did the neighbors have any problems with the applicant?

6. Were the police ever involved with the applicant on the property?

7. Would you rent to the applicant again?

Background Check

If the applicant has never rented before, or you were not able to get satisfactory answers from the past landlord, you may want to consider getting a background check of the applicant. Companies that provide background checks can be found in the yellow pages. These checks take about three to 10 business days to complete.

As with a credit check, you will need to have your applicant's social security number and permission to conduct a background check.

Applicant Interview

A good way to determine the character of an applicant is to talk with them directly. Ask them questions while filling in their rent application. In this way, you can see how they answer and if they look uncomfortable with any of the questions.

This strategy also gives the applicant a chance to clear up any possible information that might turn up in a credit or background check. For instance, if they were late on their rent for two months during a work related injury, you would feel more at ease with the information.

Been There, Done That.

Marilyn Currie, CSP, of Chilliwack, B.C. Canada, has the following true story of an investment she had. It is a cautionary tale to all investors:

'Police invade home in residential neighborhood' scream the headlines, and a breathless announcer tells the world on the evening news. Unfortunately, the homeowners did not see the evening news and no one informed them, not even the police or the neighbors.

Kids trying to break into the property told police of the pot growing operation. Police got the required documents, waited for the renter to return, and arrested him. Police then disconnected the electricity and water, confiscated the marijuana, and left. The grower was caught with cocaine in his truck, but was charged and released with a promise to appear in court at another date.

April 1 (April Fools' Day) the homeowner arrived to pick up the rent check and found a disaster. The back door was propped shut with a large board, the keys did not work in the locks, and there was no sign of the renter.

Apparently, the renter had moved back into the house and lived there for two weeks without utilities. The mess that greeted the owner was disgusting. One room was filled with garbage from floor to ceiling, hydroponics equipment covered floors and ceilings, the plumbing was plugged with dirt, and huge holes had been cut into the walls and floors to allow for ventilation.

The insurance company refused payment as they stated it was a criminal act and the perpetrator was given a fine and released.

Repairs were completed and the house sold at a loss. From the original down payment, loss of income, repair costs, and expected future profits, a total of $80,000 was lost.

Do a criminal check on the renter. It is your property and your investment, and you must be a good steward of that investment.

YOUR STANDARDS

You will want to know what standards you are looking for in a tenant. After you have gathered the information, you need to compare that information to the standards you have set. Such standards include the following:

Income: Set a minimum income, maximum income ratio, or maximum debt ratio.

Employment: Set a minimum time for employment at the same job. Most lenders require at least two years at a particular job.

Residence: Determine how long the applicant was at their last residence (many landlords require at least two years).

Evictions: Determine whether you will accept an applicant who has been evicted in the past.

Complaints: Determine whether you will accept applicants who have had complaints from past landlords or neighbors.

Bad Credit: Determine whether you will accept an applicant with bad credit.

Unverifiable Information: Determine how will you handle unverifiable information.

Been There, Done That

Debbie Malone would never have guessed that the following scenario could happen to her:

"We rented a two-family unit to two sisters who did not get along. The police were there more than 20 times due to complaints over loud music and suspected drug dealing and prostitution. We never received a call, so talk to the neighbors; if you suspect something, check the police records. They were way behind in rent, dangling the 'accident settlement any day' carrot in front of my husband who took pity on one sister.

"They finally moved, owing thousands in rent. A few months later, we read about the quiet sister who broke into someone's house and attempted to kill them. She was sentenced to more than 70 years in prison."

THE APPLICATION PROCESS

When you know the standards you wish to follow and how you plan to find out the information that will help you get tenants with those standards, you need to think about the application process. Here are a few tips:

Treat applicants with fairness: You will need to follow the same procedure with each applicant interested in your vacancy. The best way to ensure fairness, and to help the applicants see that you are being fair, is to put your application policies in writing.

Require an application: Having an application will ensure that you get all the information you need to make a good decision regarding the applicant. Include the following on the application:

- Current address and phone number

- Social security number

- Length of time at current address

- Names and phone numbers of past landlords

- Name, address, and phone number of current employer

- Current income — salary and all other sources to be considered

- References' names with phone numbers and addresses

- Questions of importance to you, such as number of vehicles, pets, or waterbeds

- Statement authorizing you to contact references and check other provided information

- Statement authorizing you to obtain a credit report and a background check

Investor Insight: Each tenant over the age of 18 should fill out an application. If you do not check everyone who will be on the lease, you may find that, although one person has good credit, the one who has been responsible for payments in the past does not.

THE TIME HAS COME

The first thing you need to do when making the final choice for an applicant is to eliminate those who do not meet your written standards. For instance, if you want an income ratio of 33 percent, all applicants who do not meet this standard can be discarded.

After you have eliminated those applicants not meeting your criteria, you will have to decide between those who remain. Some landlords accept tenants in the order in which they applied. Others look at the applications more carefully, looking for further clues such as a glowing past landlord report as opposed to simply a good one, or an applicant who has held the same job for 10 years.

Investor Insight: If you have more than one unit, you may want to keep the applicants on file for three to six months in case another opening occurs.

After you have made the decision, you will need to let the applicant know as quickly as possible. You do not want them to find another place to live before you contact them. If you find that they have already taken another rental unit, you can move on to the next applicant on your list.

It is also important that you turn down an applicant so that they can continue their search elsewhere. If you have turned down the applicant due to something found on the credit check, you need to give them the name of the credit bureau that provided the report. A letter you can give to such applicants is provided in the Appendix.

Finally, if you required application fees, all such fees for those applicants who were turned down must be returned. It is best to do so as quickly as possible to avoid any legal problems from applicants stating that you kept their money for a longer period than necessary.

CASE STUDY: DEBBIE MALONE

Debbie Malone is a realtor and a real estate investor. When it comes to finding tenants, she is aware of the difficulties it can present.

When asked how she gets good tenants, Debbie replied, "We advertise in the newspaper and our work newsletter and by word of mouth from other tenants, but it is hit or miss. You can do all the right research, but sometimes it just does not turn out right. That is why I use a lease. In this way, if I rent to a bad tenant and end up in court, I have documentation to help with my case."

Debbie uses a standard lease found at her local office supply store and says that despite being generic, it is sufficient for her needs; but she does agree that if you have specific issues you want to address, having a lawyer draft, or at least review, the lease before having a tenant sign is a good idea.

One way that Debbie helps to recoup any losses to a poor tenant is by collecting a deposit up front. Her policy is to collect a deposit equal to one month's rent. "If rent is $900 per month, we ask for the same amount for security. We tell them verbally and in writing that this is not last month's rent, it is insurance against damages. If the tenant moves without damaging the property, they get their full security back." If, however, the tenant leaves without paying rent or leaves with damages, the deposit will cover at least some of the cost.

CASE STUDY: DEBBIE MALONE

Another thing that Debbie does to help encourage on-time payments is to charge a late fee. Rent is due on the first of each month and a late fee of $25 is charged after the fifth of each month. The lease states that being late three times in their lease period constitutes a breach of the lease agreement and the tenant will be asked to move.

Debbie says, "Make sure you tell them verbally and in writing what your policy is when you fill out the lease. Stick to it. We remind tenants that we have a mortgage to pay and if they do not pay rent on time, we have to come up with that payment from another source.

"We are not, however, without feeling when it comes to the payment of the rent. If the tenant is good and responsible and they hit a rough patch (medical bills or layoff), we work with them to allow them to stay even though they may owe back rent. As long as they are making the effort and they are up front, we give them a break.

"We had a tenant who was laid off and got behind on rent. We worked with him for a year to get him on his feet. Two years later, he bought the house from us. It was a win-win for all.

"We had one tenant who rented for seven years, and another for 10 years. We have a Section 8 tenant who does the best she can and she has been in the property for several years now. If you treat people well and help when you can, they respect you and treat your property well and try to do well by you.

"However, if you have tenants who are behind on rent and are avoiding you, they are not working with you and they need to go. Get them out as soon as possible. Keep up with the correspondence and document everything.

"We have evicted several tenants over the years. It is nerve wracking the first few times, but it is not a bad process in Virginia. If rent is not received by the 5th, we send a demand for rent letter. If we have not received rent in full, plus late fee within five days, we file with the court and the sheriff serves the tenant. Most tenants receive the letter and move out before the court date. If it goes to court, most tenants do not bother to show up in court and the judge automatically rules in our favor.

"If the tenant does show up on the court date, the judge asks the tenant if they owe the money, and the judge says pay your landlord and get out in X days or the sheriff will physically remove you from the property.

"After the judgment, we go over to the sheriff's office for an eviction date. We have only had one tenant whom the sheriff had to remove. I think the tenant was shocked that they were being removed and they had not packed. The sheriff gave them five

CASE STUDY: DEBBIE MALONE

minutes to get whatever they wanted and waited for them to leave and told them not to return to the property. They were told to make arrangements with the landlord to remove their belongings. If they were not removed with 24 hours, their belongings became ours.

"We did have to go back that night because the tenant broke into the house. The police came and chased him out. They never called and we removed anything of value and sold it to recoup rent owed."

Despite having a few problem tenants, Debbie believes that real estate is a good investment. "Over the past 25 years, we have invested in the stock market and lost money, bought CDs and lost money, and invested in bonds and lost money. Nothing has given the return on investment that owning real estate has. We have purchased more than 45 properties, have never lost money on any of them, and we feel it is the safest place to invest our money."

Even in a soft market, she believes that real estate is a good investment. Others may be scared off and afraid of buying, and that is when you can potentially make a great purchase. "You can find undervalued property, fix it up, rent it for a few years, and turn a nice profit when the market improves. As far as I am concerned, there is no right time or wrong time to buy rental properties. It is about being able to locate the right deal and the right property for us and knowing where to look for it."

Even though Debbie owns 45 properties, she is a hands-on landlord, collecting the rent, doing the bookkeeping, and providing general maintenance, including painting and landscaping. Due to liability, she subs out any electrical and HVAC work and any complicated plumbing. She also contracts out roofers and contractors for larger repairs.

"When we purchase a property, we assess what it needs. We check the hot water heater. Many times the elements need to be replaced, and sometimes the unit leaks. We find it better to spend the money up front and replace the unit (around $200) instead of having the tenant place a $75 service call.

"We check the plumbing fixtures, replace leaking faucets and outdated light fixtures, and change batteries in smoke detectors and make sure they are in working order.

"When we rent the property, we go over a property condition checklist with the new tenant. We list flaws and defects and have them sign a document regarding condition so we are all in agreement as to the condition. We also take photos. It is amazing how many times a tenant moves out and they say they did not damage the wall, carpet, or linoleum. If the condition is listed when they move in, it saves much aggravation when they leave.

CASE STUDY: DEBBIE MALONE

"After a renter has moved out, we go in and assess the condition again. We allow for normal wear and tear, but if the property was just painted a year before and there are handprints all over the walls, if it is dirty, or there is damage or stains to carpeting, we assess a fee for repairs from their security deposit."

Debbie mentions two mistakes you need to avoid with your units. One is forgoing the annual or bi-annual inspections. You need to inspect your properties and address the problems as they come up. Do not wait until the tenant is moving out to make them pay for damages. If they break something a month into the lease, they should pay for it then.

The other mistake to avoid is forgoing the move-in inspection with the tenant. If you do not have documentation on the state of the unit, you will not be able to hold tenants to the repairs you have to do when they move.

Debbie understands the need for a good team of people for her investment business and she understands that good subcontractors need to be on that team. In addition to subcontractors, such as a roofer, flooring installer, sheetrock finisher, and vinyl siding installer, Debbie has an accountant, an attorney, a settlement company, an insurance company, and a loan officer. She is her own realtor, but suggests that those investors who are not realtors should seek one out.

As a realtor, Debbie feels pretty confident when choosing a property. "If it is in a decent location and has curb appeal, we can expect to have a good experience with renters and that the property will appreciate. Having access to property info, I can assess whether it will be a good property or not.

"Location is the number one consideration. Physical condition is next. I always want to know how much money I will have to invest to bring it up to the condition we want. Price is third, and it can be negotiated based on the needs of the property.

"Being a realtor gives me an edge when finding a property, but the MLS is the number one way we find property. HUD and bank-owned (REO) foreclosure Web sites are the second and word of mouth/FSBO are the third. We do not buy at auctions anymore, too much competition and the prices are driven up sometimes over what the property would have sold for on MLS."

Since Debbie understands real estate and the market trends in her area, she has invested in rental and flipped properties. "Some properties we buy with the intention of flipping, while others are long-term rentals. We just bought one property because it had a large detached garage and a ½ acre lot. We have been looking for such a property to store all of our rental equipment in one location. We bought another

CASE STUDY: DEBBIE MALONE

because it was in a neighborhood that our teenage daughter would like to live in one day. We used it as a 1031; it will keep paying itself down and we can gift it to her, avoiding the taxes."

Debbie believes that fixer-uppers can work for long-term investments and for flipping, depending on how much time you have to invest to bring the property up to a standard that would sell quickly. "If it requires much work that you have to hire out, it can cut into your profit. If it is more of a cosmetic update, you can get in and out quickly and flip it. I like the long-term investments that you can take your time on and make a profit and work at your pace."

Debbie Malone, ABR, e-PRO, ASP
RE/MAX 1st Olympic Realtors
malone1981@aol.com
www.debmalone.com
434-546-0369

When you have chosen your tenant, it is time to have them sign the lease. In Chapter 10, we will explore the lease and the clauses and disclosures necessary to make your business more successful.

10

THE FINE PRINT

When it comes to landlord-tenant relationships, the lease is where it all begins. A lease or rental agreement is a contract between a landlord and a tenant. The contract gives the tenant the right to live on the property for a specific time.

A lease explains all the tenant's and landlord's rights and responsibilities. It states the terms of the lease including rent, length of tenancy, and any other rules specific to the property. A typical lease runs for one year, during which time the rent must remain the same and the tenant cannot move out unless you agree to the move.

A rental agreement is similar to a lease but does not specify a time. If you use a month-to-month rental agreement, you can change the rent with proper notification and the tenant can move elsewhere with proper notification.

WRITTEN VERSUS ORAL

There are two different types of leases — oral and written. Although both kinds of leases are legal as long as it does not extend beyond one year, it is wise to enter into a written lease or agreement.

An oral agreement can easily lead to misunderstandings and even problems over the enforcement of terms. You may have told the tenant that you will not allow pets, but if you did not write it down, you have no proof of that clause. Even the amount of rent your tenant is paying could be argued.

A written agreement means that the terms of the lease are bound by law and can be documented as such. A written lease provides you with the legal basis for enforcing the obligations of the tenant.

Investor Insight: Make sure that everyone over the age of 18 who will live in the unit signs the lease.

WHAT TO INCLUDE

The content of your lease is up to you, with the exception of federal, state, and local laws regarding what leases can and cannot say. To learn of these laws before writing your lease, contact the governmental office in your municipality or county that handles landlord/tenant relations.

Most leases include the following information:

- Name and signature of landlord

- Name and signature of all tenants

- Date of signing

- Address of the unit rented

- The beginning and ending dates of the lease

- The rent amount and due date

- Procedure for collecting rent and late fees

- Returned check fees

- Security deposit and advance rent

- How security deposits will be returned

- Policy concerning security deposit as last month's rent

- Notice required to terminate the lease and where notices should be sent

- Disclosures such as lead based paint

A sample lease is available in the Appendix. Please note that this lease is for sample purposes only. Before you use this or any other lease, be sure that it meets your state and local requirements.

BECAUSE OF THE CLAUSE

Many items listed on the lease are clauses. These are special items that are not true of all rental properties and may not even be true of each one of your properties. You have to be sure that any special policies you add meet with state and local laws. For instance, some states do not allow landlords to collect first or last month's rent. Others have deposit maximum limits.

You also cannot ask tenants to give up their rights. They have the right to have a safe environment with heat that allows no water to come in. They also have the right to get back unused portions of their deposit and be given warning before you enter the premises. Therefore, your lease will not hold up in court if you have asked your tenants to give up such basic rights.

You can require tenants to behave in certain ways as long as it is done within the law. For instance, you can ask them to keep the unit safe, keep it sanitary, or park in designated spots. You can also ask them to refrain from acting in certain ways, such as making noise that disturbs the neighbors, keeping pets, or using a grill on the balcony.

When you know the laws, you are free to choose the specifications of your lease. You may want to consider the following clauses:

Pets — Stipulate whether you allow pets and, if so, what kind.

Late rent payment — Stipulate the fine associated with late rent. You will need to address the actual due date of rent payments and the grace period before a late charge is assessed. You may also specify how many times a tenant can be late before more serious consequences occur.

Services as part of rent — State whether the rent includes water, electric, garbage collection, and/or phone service.

Renovation policy — State whether the tenant may paint, add wallpaper, put up railing, or add walls. Cosmetic changes are often allowed while major renovations are not.

Subletting policy — Stipulate whether subletting is permitted and whether it requires your approval.

Repairs — Explain to the tenant what to do in case a repair is needed. You can also lay out who is responsible for which repairs and any fees associated with specific repairs.

Renter's insurance — Stipulate whether you require renter's insurance.

Right of Entry — Detail when and how a landlord can enter a tenant's home.

Waterbeds — Stipulate whether you will allow a waterbed and whether it can be on the second floor. You can also stipulate that the renter must pay for all water damage due to a defective waterbed.

Others possible clauses include the following:

- Number of people per unit

- Parking policies

- Policy regarding illegal activity

- Attorney fees for evictions

To find wording for clauses such as these, you can go to **http://www. buyincomeproperties.com/FreeRealEstateForms.htm#rentaladden**.

WRITTEN IN STONE, UNLESS...

Although you have signed and dated a lease, you are able to make changes after it is signed. For instance, your tenant may have signed the lease and then decided to get married. She will need to change her lease to indicate her new last name and to add her spouse to the lease. Your tenant may be sent to another job location and need to sublet the apartment.

Any change can be made as long as it is done in writing and agreed on by you and your tenant. A sample letter stating a change in the lease is in the Appendix.

HIRING THE BIG GUN

As a real estate investor, you should make use of professionals who know their end of your business. One example would be the use of an attorney when writing up your lease template.

You can buy a template in any store, but you may find that the standard agreement does not work for you.

Investor Insight: When you make a modification to an existing lease, make sure that all the blank lines are either completed or deleted. If you write in changes, they need to be initialed by you and by the tenant.

It is a good idea to hire an attorney who specializes in real estate law to prepare a lease for you, or at least look over the lease you have drawn up. Ask other landlords who they use. You can also get referrals from your real estate agent or your lender.

CASE STUDY: DAWN COOK

Dawn Cook is a home stager and real estate investor in Indiana. Dawn finds her good tenants by screening carefully. Once she has a tenant in place, she keeps them happy by responding to their needs, keeping the rent fair, and giving them their privacy. If she has a bad tenant, Dawn says to "get your lawyer on it right away and get them out ASAP. I do not mess around with bad tenants That can be a nightmare that will not end."

Dawn discusses a standard lease versus one drawn up by her attorney. "I have used both and I will never use a standard lease again because there are too many liabilities; I have had an attorney who specializes in real estate law draw mine up. Be careful to choose a lawyer with experience and knowledge in this field."

The lease that Dawn uses with her tenants explains her security deposit policy. "I always get a security deposit of the full rent plus a $200 cleaning deposit; both are refundable 'if' the place is found clean and in good order. If everything is okay after the tenant moves out, both will be returned within 30 days after they leave the premises.

"I also explain my late payment policy. I do not want to encourage late rent payments, so I charge them $25 per day for the first day and $20 per day every day after until it is paid in full."

When Dawn had to evict someone, she was thankful to have her lease and her lawyer handy. "I contacted my lawyer and had her handle it. I answered one call from the

CASE STUDY: DAWN COOK

tenant and directed her to contact my attorney and informed her I would no longer be receiving her calls. My lawyer sent her a letter informing her to make any and all contact to her only (in accordance with the lease) and my lawyer got her out. It was a pain, but I am glad that I had a good lawyer I could trust to take care of it for me. I cannot imagine how horrible it would be to do it by myself.

Dawn shares her feelings about real estate investing. "I believe if you make good choices and are well informed, investing in real estate is an excellent way to make awesome amounts of money no matter what your education level, status, or gender."

Dawn Cook
Staged to Sell
219-513-8945
http://activerain.com/dawnc
stagedtosellquick@comcast.net

LEAD PAINT DISCLOSURE

Since this information is so important, and so costly if done incorrectly, the information concerning the lead paint disclosure comes directly from the HUD Web site.

Congress passed the Residential Lead-Based Paint Hazard Reduction Act of 1992, also known as Title X, to protect families from exposure to lead from paint, dust, and soil. Section 1018 of this law directed HUD and EPA to require the disclosure of known information on lead-based paint and lead-based paint hazards before the sale or lease of most housing built before 1978.

Before ratification of a contract for housing sale or lease, sellers and landlords must do the following:

- Give an EPA-approved information pamphlet on identifying and controlling lead-based paint hazards ("Protect Your Family From Lead In Your Home" pamphlet, currently available in English, Spanish, Vietnamese, Russian, Arabic and Somali).

- Disclose any known information concerning lead-based paint or lead-based paint hazards. The seller or landlord must also disclose information such as the location of the lead-based paint and/ or lead-based paint hazards, and the condition of the painted surfaces.

- Provide any records and reports on lead-based paint and/or lead-based paint hazards, which are available to the seller or landlord (for multi-unit buildings, this requirement includes records and reports concerning common areas and other units, when such information was obtained as a result of a building-wide evaluation).

- Include an attachment to the contract or lease, or language inserted in the lease itself, which includes a Lead Warning Statement and confirms that the seller or landlord has complied with all notification requirements. This attachment is to be provided in the same language used in the rest of the contract. Sellers or landlords, agents, and homebuyers or tenants must sign and date the attachment.

- Sellers must provide homebuyers a 10-day period to conduct a paint inspection or risk assessment for lead-based paint or lead-based paint hazards. Parties may mutually agree, in writing, to lengthen or shorten the time period for inspection. Homebuyers may waive this inspection opportunity.

You can download a copy of "Protect Your Family From Lead in Your Home" at **http://www.hud.gov/utilities/intercept.cfm?/offices/lead/ outreach/pyf_eng.pdf.**

FOLLOW THE LAW — ALL OF THEM

As a landlord, you are responsible for knowing state, local, and federal laws and regulations that have to do with rental properties. Failure to comply with a law can cost you fines or even lawsuits.

State laws deal with the following:

- Security deposits
- Housing standards
- Repairs and maintenance
- Landlord right of entry
- Rental rules
- Evictions

State laws that affect landlords can be obtained from your state's Consumer Protection Agency or Attorney General's Office. You can also find them at the library; in some states, they are available online.

Two good ways to find state statutes are to use a search engine specific to laws, such as **www.findlaw.com**, or to go to the Cornell University Web site, **www.law.cornell.edu/states/index.html**, where they maintain a database of state statutes.

Investor Insight: Check for updates regularly, as laws can change whenever your state government is in session.

Local laws and ordinances should also be obtained. Local housing codes deal with the following:

- Structural requirements
- Health and safety standards
- Plumbing standards
- Heating standards

These laws can be found at your local building or housing authority, health department, fire department, or city manager or mayor's office.

In addition to the state and local laws, you need to be familiar with the federal laws. Federal laws include the following:

- Discrimination

- Environmental health hazards

- Landlord responsibilities

You can find these laws in the U.S. Code or in the Code of Federal Regulations. Access it online at **www.law.cornell.edu**.

FAIR HOUSING LAWS

The Fair Housing Act (FHA) is the main piece of legislation that regulates multi-family rentals. It began as a way to provide fair housing throughout the United States by prohibiting discrimination.

The Fair Housing Act stipulates that no one can deny access to housing based on the following:

- Race
- Color
- Religion

- Sex
- Familial status
- Handicap

- National origin

States often have their own Fair Housing Acts that go beyond that of the federal government, including the following:

- Age
- Sexual orientation

- Personal appearance
- Political affiliation

- Place of residence
- Matriculation

- Veteran status

In addition to the lease of real estate, the law includes such things as advertising, interviewing of applicants, acceptance criteria, and renewal criteria.

Here are four steps you can take to stay in the bounds of the FHA:

1. Make policies based on wise business decisions.

2. Have all your policies in writing.

3. Let others who work for you know your policies and teach them how you want those policies to be carried out.

4. Be consistent — you must treat all applicants equally.

ARE YOU INSURED?

As a landlord, you are responsible for the safety of your unit. You can also be held liable for any accidents that occur. Therefore, it is in your best interest to have good insurance.

If you already have insurance, you may want to check your coverage to be sure that it deals with things common to investment property.

As with any insurance, there are differences in landlord policies and in the prices of these policies, but any policy you choose should include the following items:

- **Malicious damage by tenant** — This is all intentional damage to walls, doors, floors, ceilings, and outside structures.

- **Accidental damage** — This includes all those things that happen by accident, such as a washcloth getting flushed down the toilet by a two-year-old.

- **Legal liability** — This is for expenses due to lawsuits, for expenses rising from a tenant who got hurt, or from property damage or loss.

- **Loss of rental income** — Sometimes damage, whether malicious or accidental, results in a loss of income while the property is restored to order. Loss of income can also happen if tenants default on their payments, if hardship is granted to a tenant by the court, or upon the death of a sole tenant.

Insurance premiums look expensive at first, but when you realize how much they can do for you, the price is well worth it.

There are many different types of insurance you can choose from. You will not need them all, but you do need at least liability insurance to cover you if someone is hurt on your property. You should also have basic property insurance to cover losses from fire or theft.

Other insurances you may want to consider include the following:

- **Tenant relocation insurance** — This will help your tenants with a move if your property becomes uninhabitable due to a disaster.

- **Flood insurance**

- **Bonding** — This will protect you against loss if you or someone you hire is robbed while they have rent money on them.

With the lease signed and the insurance in place, you will become a landlord. From that time forth, you will need to know how to keep your tenants happy and understand the administrative side of the business. In Chapter 11, you will learn about managing your tenants.

11

DOT THE I'S AND CROSS THE T'S

WELCOME, WELCOME

Your job as a landlord is to have a professional relationship with your tenants.

This process begins when you have the tenant sign a lease. At this point, you need to be sure that your tenant understands the lease. Reviewing the lease is best done on a one-on-one basis, where you can answer any questions and listen to any concerns. One thing you can do to make your tenants aware of your expectations is to orient them to the property.

For instance, show them the different rooms and make sure they know how to use the appliances. Show them the breaker box and the water cut off valve in case of emergencies. Review the area's service, such as garbage collection, newspaper, recycling, and local utilities. Give them your number so that they know how to get in touch with you. All these things will help you get started on the right foot with your tenants.

While you are showing them around, it is a good time to perform a joint inspection of the unit. This way you can both identify the condition of the unit and write it down, as well as the working order of the rooms and the appliances in the rooms. After you have written down everything, you should each sign and date the list. A sample walk-through list is provided in the Appendix.

If there are items on the list that need to be fixed, get to them as soon as possible. After you have fixed an item, you can either check mark the item on the list and have the tenant initial and date it, or you can create a new list of repairs that can be signed and dated.

Investor Insight: Keep the original list and give your tenant a copy for their records. You might also want to take photographs of the condition of the house.

When your tenant moves out, this checklist will be your evidence as to the condition before they arrived versus how the unit looks now. This checklist will help you explain why you kept part or all of the security deposit.

Keep the original and provide the tenant with a copy. Be sure to update the checklist as repairs are made to the unit, indicating the work done and the date that the repair was made. You and the tenant should initial any changes to the original checklist. When the tenant moves out, this checklist may serve as documentation or evidence as to why you withheld all or a part of a security deposit.

KEEPING IT STRAIGHT

You have used a lease and a walk-through checklist. You have also collected the deposit and the first month's rent. It is time for a good record-keeping system.

For each tenant you have, you will want to keep a record. These records should have the following:

1. Rental application

2. Credit information collected during the application process

3. Signed lease

4. Signed inspection list

5. Payment history records

6. Repair completions

7. Any mail or e-mail correspondence

8. Complaints

9. Repair requests

10. Records of conversations

You may need any of the financial documents for tax time; also, the documentation between you and your tenant can be used if you ever have to go to court over a landlord/tenant issue.

You will also need to keep business records. These records will help you do your taxes, determine whether a property is performing well, and determine when you can afford another property.

Such records include the following:

- Advertising
- Car and truck expenses
- Insurance
- Office expenses

- Repair and maintenance receipts
- Contract labor
- Interest paid
- Supplies

- Taxes
- Utilities
- Wages
- Postage
- Computer hardware and software
- Legal and professional services
- Any other expenses related to your business

You can keep all your files on the computer or you can create a paper system. Something as easy as an expandable file will work for receipts and a running total on rents paid. Or you can have a specific real estate investor software to do it all for you. Whatever you choose, just be sure that you keep everything and know where you keep it.

HAND IT OVER... PLEASE

As per your lease agreement, your tenants will know how much rent will be charged each month. They will also know when it is due and where the payments can be made. As a landlord, you will have to decide which forms of payment you feel comfortable accepting — cash, check, money order, or any of the three.

> **Investor Insight:** If you accept cash, be sure to give the tenant a written receipt that has their name, the amount paid, and the date it was paid.

There are many different ways to collect the rent. One is personal collection, meaning that you go by each tenant's home and have them hand the rent to you directly. Personal collection often means that you have to set appointments and then hope that the tenant is there at the appointed time. The advantage is that you see the money immediately and know exactly who has paid and who has not.

You can also have your tenants drop off the payments in a drop box of some sort or at an office location. Be sure to specify exactly where the drop off is located and who can accept the check.

Having your tenants put the rent in the mail is also an option. The problem is that you are depending on the postal service to get the check to you. Tenants will put the check in the mail a day or two after it is due and it will not arrive for several days, or they will say that they put the check in the mail when they did not. The advantage is that it is a low-hassle way to collect the rent.

You may also provide your tenants with a deposit slip that they will take directly to the bank along with their payment. In this way, the payment is deposited immediately and you do not have to go to the bank to take care of it.

If you have a large enough tenant base, you might want to consider offering a draft service where you are able to draft their account at the first of each month for the rent amount.

Been There Done That

Debbie Malone has a horror story to tell about people they believed to be good tenants:

"We had a cute ranch on an acre in the county that we did a lease/purchase for. Every month the tenant would bring $700 rent in cash to our house. I told my husband he should go by the property once in a while to check on it and he thought if the guy was dropping off $700 cash, there would not be a problem. That was a big mistake!

"One day the tenant called and said they were moving because they could not buy the house. My husband went by and it was a disaster.

"Dirty is one thing — this was filthy. There were three layers of carpet in the living room all soaked with dog urine and feces. We had to have the floors refinished and sealed four times. In the basement laundry room, they left over two feet of wet, rotting clothing. There were needles strewn all over the inside and outside the house (he had hepatitis C — no wonder).

"The worst was the master bedroom. This home had an addition with a nice deck. The tenant thought this would be a perfect spot to tie their pet goat up. There was a foot of goat pellets that had to be shoveled out, by me. It was so gross."

SO LONG, FAREWELL

No matter how good of a landlord you are, you are going to have some tenants leave. That is simply the nature of the business.

If you have a month-to-month lease, the tenant should notify you in writing that they are going to leave. Your lease will have stated the terms of this notice, which is most often 30 days. If they do not give you notice, they will be obligated to pay rent for a full 30 days after leaving.

If you collected the last month's rent when the tenant rented the unit, by law you have to use this money for their last month.

If you have a longer lease and the tenant wishes to move, you have three choices:

- You can insist that they honor the lease by staying there or by paying for the unit until the lease is up.

- You can allow them to sublet their unit to someone else for the term of the lease.

- You can rewrite the lease to a month-to-month lease, allow them to give the 30-day notice, and then move.

After a tenant has stayed in a unit for the lease period, they have the option of moving. Most landlords specify in the original lease agreement that tenants will need to give a 60-day notice before the lease expiration of their intent to move when the lease is up.

If they do not intend to move, you can either have them sign a new lease or convert to a month-to-month lease.

Investor Insight: In most states, if you accept rent after the lease has expired, you have automatically created a month-to-month lease. If you do not wish to go month-to-month, have the tenant sign a new lease before accepting any rent payments beyond the lease term.

Just as you followed a certain procedure when your tenant moved in, you need to follow one when they move out. You will want to let the tenant know how you will inspect the property, what deductions you will make from the security deposit for what repairs, and how you will get the remainder of the security deposit to them.

After the tenant has moved out their belongings and cleaned the unit, you will want to inspect for cleanliness standards and for necessary repairs. If you have the tenant do this inspection with you, they will know how much is being charged and why. Then have the tenant sign the report.

When you return the deposit to the tenant, send it to their forwarding mail address with a note detailing the initial deposit, the amounts deducted, and the purpose of those deductions.

LET US TALK THIS OVER

As a landlord, understand that disputes with tenants are inevitable, but there are things you can do to keep these disputes to a minimum:

1. **Know the law.** Many disputes happen because one party or the other does not know the law. You may have written an illegal lease policy, or the tenant may not understand their obligation to follow the lease. It may even be something as simple as the tenant not understanding a particular clause in the lease.

2. **Stay calm.** Even if your tenant is screaming, you should remain professional.

3. **Discuss it.** You will be amazed how quickly some issues can be resolved simply by discussing them. There may be an easy solution to the problem.

4. **Meet with the tenant.** Rather than starting out with your lawyer, try talking with your tenant one-on-one.

5. **Get a mediator.** A mediator is a neutral third party who helps you and your tenant work out your differences. Some courts offer this service for free and sometimes Housing Commissioners have the authority to help.

6. **Get an arbitrator.** The arbitrator is also a neutral third party, but unlike a mediator, an arbitrator has the right to make the final decision. In binding arbitration, you agree before the start of the process that you will abide by whatever the arbitrator decides.

7. **Save everything.** Keep a record of everything that pertains to the situation. Any letters written, dates of any face-to-face meetings, police reports, or anything that will prove your case.

8. **Turn it over to a lawyer.** If doing all you can do has not worked, call your lawyer. Often, just getting a lawyer involved will end the dispute without it ever having to go to court.

THE CHECK IS NOT IN THE MAIL

One of the biggest problems you will run into is nonpayment of rent. Nonpayment can also include only partial payment of rent and any assessed late charges.

If the rent is not paid on time, you must follow a legal procedure to get it. If you do not, and the time comes that legal proceedings must be held, you can end up in trouble with the law instead of your tenant.

Start by sending a late rent notice immediately after the grace period has expired. The late notice should inform the tenant of any late fees associated with his/her tardiness in payment.

If you do not hear from the tenant within two to four days of sending the notice, it is time to call the tenant. Let them know that their late fees are adding up. Also tell them when the account will automatically go to your attorney for eviction proceedings.

If you get no response, you can send a warning letter from the attorney asking them to pay all rent by a specified day to avoid an eviction.

If the tenant still does not respond, you will have to start the eviction process. You can also report your tenant to the credit bureau reporting agencies.

GET OUT... NOW

You may have the best tenant screening process in the world, and yet you will have to evict someone. Eviction is the legal, forcible removal of a tenant from your property. Eviction is not pleasant and may well be the worst part of your job as a landlord. It is costly, it takes times, it can be complex, and it may need the services of your attorney. Despite this, sometimes eviction is necessary.

Evictions may be necessary as a result of the following tenant problems:

- Nonpayment of rent

- Refusal to follow the lease and its provisions

- Engaging in illegal activity on your property

- Creating a nuisance problem

- Refusal to leave after the lease has expired

Been There, Done That

Debbie Malone's experience with illegal activity:

"My husband was refinishing the floors at a rental. He opened a closet door and found a pot farm! He called the police who set up a raid. We gave them a key so they would not break our front door. If you know there is something illegal going on, tell the police. If you let it go, or if they think you know what was going on, they can seize your home."

Investor Insight: If your tenant is involved in illegal activity, you can call the police and have them arrested, but starting the eviction process is still up to you.

The best piece of advice for starting the eviction process is to begin immediately. The process is long enough on its own; delaying will only cost you more time. Additionally, the longer a disgruntled tenant is in the unit, the more chance you have of sustaining damage.

Evictions are often held by Small Claims Court, but in some areas, they are handled by Housing Courts or Housing Sections of Superior Courts.

Be sure to know which court your area uses before beginning the eviction process against a tenant.

Eviction processes differ from state to state, but they all follow the same basic steps. The steps listed in this section are only a guide. You need to learn the laws for your area or have your attorney handle the eviction.

Even if you choose to use an attorney, it will be helpful to understand the main steps.

Serve Notice: You will need to serve your tenant with a notice. This notice is a document that lets the tenant know that you are starting the eviction procedure. It is important that this notice be served properly, so it is best to have a sheriff or sheriff's deputy deliver it. You can also use a company that deals specifically with serving legal documents.

You will also have to have the notice delivered to the court. You will need proof that you did so.

After the tenant has received the notice, they are then called a "tenant at sufferance." When it has reached this point, the court has control of the tenancy of the tenant at sufferance. The tenant has the right to remain until the court states otherwise.

Initiate the Proceeding: The notice will state the number of days a landlord must wait between the serving of the notice and the commencement of the eviction proceeding. After this time has passed, you will need to submit a petition to the court and pay a court filing fee. The petition will explain your reason for initiating the eviction and include the amount of money you believe is owed to you.

The court then issues a notice called a summons that demands that you and your tenant show up in court on a specific day. This notice will also have the petition attached.

Wait for Response: When the summons has been received by the tenant, they have to respond to the complaint within a certain number of days. They can respond by stating that the complaint is true, or they may respond with a defense as to why the complaint is not true. Their defenses may be that they already paid the rent, that they did not receive the notice legally, that they withheld the rent because you did not make repairs, that you are retaliating because they made a complaint against you, or that you are charging more than is due.

Attend the Hearing: You must show up at the hearing. If you do not, the case may be dismissed. If your tenant does not show up, it is likely you will win your case by default. Present your facts as objectively as possible, and do so in chronological order. Do not interrupt your tenant when they are speaking and do not become argumentative. If the tenant says something untrue, make a note of it and bring it up when it is your turn to speak.

Get the Eviction Order: You will receive an order stating that you are legally allowed to remove the tenant from the property. If your tenant has appealed the judge's ruling, you may have to wait until the appeal period is over.

Remove the Tenant: You may have to have the sheriff remove the tenant from the premises. You may be required to store the evicted tenant's belongings, but this requirement varies by state, as does the length of time you need to store the items.

There are ways to make your business easier to manage, even with nonpayment of rents and evictions. The computer is one tool that can make the life of a landlord much easier. In Chapter 12, you will learn the various ways your business can be better by using a computer.

CASE STUDY: TAMMY KEMP

Tammy Kemp of Pennsylvania is a real estate investor with three properties, although she recently owned as many as seven. One reason Tammy has cut back on her rental properties is eviction.

"We do not want any more right now because, for the first time, we are encountering evicting a tenant and it has left quite a bad taste in our mouths. It is not a pleasant situation. We have found that our tenant needs to be evicted but is savvy as to how the system works. Before we take on more rentals, we will need to review our selection process and how to handle evictions more efficiently. Thankfully, we have a good attorney and recommend that anyone investing in real estate have one, too."

Despite this bad experience, Tammy wants to be an investor. She says that real estate investing will always be a good investment because people will always need a place to live. As interest rates go up and people have a harder time purchasing their own home, rental investing is even more desirable. Of course, she cautions that the only time you should buy is when the monthly rental income on the property will exceed your principal, interest, taxes, and insurance (PITI). "As for us, we never want to be put in an upside-down position."

To determine whether a house will meet the PITI requirements, Tammy and her husband split up the work. Tammy's husband determines whether the house is structurally sound. "We only buy a property if the work to be done is of a cosmetic nature."

Tammy makes the decision on the financial aspects. She and her husband decide whether the location is good. "Location is of paramount importance because that will determine the caliber of tenant willing to rent it. My husband and I keep our eyes open for signs of neglected properties and let our real estate agent know that we are always in the market if the price is right."

Since Tammy buys properties that are in good areas and in good condition, you would think she would have no trouble keeping tenants, but there are some issues. "We are in a Catch-22. We get good tenants by charging a higher than average rent in return for a better than average dwelling. However, the tenants who can afford the higher rent are usually just in between houses (renting while building a new home, relocating, etc.), so they never stay for more than a year."

Due to their choice of homes and the type of tenant these homes attract, Tammy

CASE STUDY: TAMMY KEMP

prefers to use a month-to-month lease. This way, either party can get out of the lease whenever necessary. She found a standard lease in a book of landlord forms, but will be reviewing that lease in light of her recent eviction issue.

When Tammy is notified that a tenant will be leaving, she contacts them by mail immediately. "I send them a letter explaining what we expect the property to look like when they leave. It also contains an itemized price list for any repairs, replacements, or cleaning that we may have to do and lets the tenant know that the money will be withheld from their security deposit. You would be amazed at how clean our properties are when they leave. This only works if the property is immaculate and in good working order when they first start their tenancy."

Tammy also shares how she gets her tenants to pay their rent on time. "All rents are due on the 1st of the month and we offer them a $25 discount if their rent is paid anytime before the due date. It is a win-win situation — they get to save $25 per month and we get all the rents in at one time."

For Tammy, real estate investing is fun. She is thrilled when she takes a drab home and makes it shine. She has also been blessed to meet some nice people who, after they were no longer tenants, became good friends.

Tammy Kemp
First Impressions Home Staging& Interior Redesign
http://www.1stimpressions-pa.com/
E-mail: tammykemp@epix.net
Phone: 610-863-6756
Fax: 610- 863-9532
704 Middletown Road
Pen Argyl, PA 18072

12

USING THE COMPUTER AND THE INTERNET

Computers can help you in your real estate investing business. Although not all investors will need the computer for the same things, many will find that it is a handy tool that will make their business run more smoothly.

If you do not know enough about a computer to feel comfortable, most community colleges offer courses that can teach you the basics about word processing, e-mail, and the Internet.

MAKE IT YOURSELF

One of the best uses of a computer is the word processing tool. Word processing programs allow you to type documents onto your computer and store them there. Then, when you have need of a document, you can pull it up straight from the computer.

The best part is the editing function. Let us say that you have four rental units. You use the same lease with all four except that information such as location and rent is changed for each property. With a word processor, you can take the standard lease and change the location of the property, the name of the tenant, the rent you will be charging, and you can even add or take away clauses in the lease. Then, all you do is save it as a new document and your computer will have a copy of the original lease and the newest version you created.

If it comes time to renew a lease, you can take out the old one, put in the correct dates and rent, save it, and print it out in a matter of minutes.

You can also create new documents, such as a tenant letter over a particular concern or a late payment letter. Once again, you can save these and make changes any time you wish.

RECORD KEEPING

Another good function of the computer is record keeping. As a landlord, you will have many receipts to keep up with that will create a record of your income versus your expenses. Computer programs specifically designed for landlords, or even simple Excel spreadsheets, will simplify keeping up with all those.

There are many different software programs that can help your business with its accounting. These programs can help you keep up with expenses, income, bank balances, depreciation, tax records, and even help you keep your own income and expenses separate from that of your business. One of the most well-known and easiest to learn is Intuit Quicken, most commonly known as Quicken.

If you want a program specifically designed for rental investing, you can check your local computer store. Most software programs such as these cost under $100.

Investor Insight: Before you buy an accounting program, make sure the data you enter into the program is compatible with the software program your CPA uses at tax time.

ARE YOU CONNECTED?

The Internet is an incredible way to have vast amounts of information at your fingertips. You can find Section 8 Housing requirements, low-cost energy saving tips, and stories of other landlords dealing with bad tenants, all on the Internet.

But the Internet can do much more than just be a glorified library.

CASE STUDY: DUAYNE WEIR

Duayne Weir, a real estate agent, investor, and contractor, believes strongly that a computer is a tool that you should use if in the business of real estate investing. "I have three Web sites — one for real estate as a realtor, one for investment real estate, and one for my contracting business. Today, if you do not have a Web site for your business, you are missing out on a presence on the Web, a virtual storefront, and the opportunity for people to do research and find you credible! A Web site will help you be a success no matter what your business — real estate or otherwise. I enjoy building Web sites and I think they should be a part of your real estate business; they will add credibility and profitability to your bottom line."

Duayne also uses his computer to keep track of income, expenses, and even to determine ROI using a property analysis software program when looking at a particular property. "We use our software to tell us what looks good on paper. Of course, there is always some risk and some unknowns. My advice is just do your due diligence going into an investment, and always have an exit strategy."

Duayne finds his investment deals on the Internet. He understands that it is a valuable research tool that will save him time.

Duayne is involved in real estate investing because he believes it is the best way to invest. "Real estate is always a good investment. You always have an insured asset, unlike in the stock market. And unlike the stock market, you can always borrow against it. Any time is a good time to buy, but I actually like to buy when the market is soft. I find that there is much inventory and the pricing is low. The downside, of course, is that financing is tough during the slow times."

As a realtor and contractor, Duayne meets several of the requirements for investment team membership. However, he does not limit himself to his own expertise. "I work with

CASE STUDY: DUAYNE WEIR

other agents and we mainly work with builders on new construction. I also work with several good mortgage bankers. I am a member of pre-paid legal, which does save me time and money when it comes to lawyers fees."

Other members on Duayne's team include a management company and subcontractors. One of the most important members of Duayne's team is a real estate tax accountant. "The tax benefits of real estate investing are the best of any investment out there, bar none. The government wants it that way so we will invest in real estate, because our whole economy revolves around real estate."

Duayne also understands that real estate investing is a good way to use retirement funds. "As long as you have a self-directed IRA and take full advantage of the 1031 exchange programs, using retirement funds makes sense. The most important thing, though, is to make sure you have the right professional assisting you."

Duayne Weir
Investment Realities LLC
Real Estate Investment Specialist
E-mail: duayne@investmentrealities.com
www.investmentrealities.com
www.duayneweir.com
Cell: 612-363-2739

Buy It, Sell It, Rent It

The Internet is a wonderful way to find properties to buy and to sell properties you are letting go. You will have the option of searching national and local sites that are databanks of property for sale. These sites are updated at least daily, and they can give you information faster than more traditional methods like the newspaper classifieds.

You can also get a better feel for the properties online than you can via print because words and photos are rather limited in print. Online advertising, however, gives the seller a chance to show multiple photos, give extensive details, display video tours, interactive maps, and more to help you make a decision to see the home in person. By the time you finish looking at an online ad, you feel as if you have been to your first showing of the home.

If you have a piece of property for sale, you can give potential buyers all the information you would want if you were in their position. By the time they contact you, they are interested. This strategy keeps you from showing the home to those who are not as interested.

As stated earlier in the book, advertising online for tenants is a good way to get tenants quickly and inexpensively. Those who are looking for a place to rent, especially if you are renting to those 40 and under, will be looking online.

Supply buying is another use for the Internet. Many stores offer online catalogs where you can place an order and have the products shipped right to your door. If you are in need of hardware, tools, or other items related to your investment business, ordering online may be a good place to start.

Some sites that may be of interest to a landlord include the following:

- **www.sears.com**

- **www.homedepot.com**

- **www.lowes.com**

- **www.walmart.com**

- **www.eBay.com**

Finances and the Web

Online banking has improved considerably over the past five years.

- You can check your account daily to see what checks have cleared and what deposits have been put in.

- You can pay your bills without ever writing a check.

- You can transfer funds between accounts.

- You can balance your checkbook.

- You can open a checking or savings account.

- You can order checks.

- You can even get pre-approved for a loan.

Another big plus with online banking is that you can compare your current loan with new loan rates to determine whether refinancing is right for you. Online financial calculators make it easy to decide. You goal is to maximize your investment, so any refinancing that will help you achieve this goal is something you should consider.

Check Them Out

Learning as much as you can about your applicants is important. Using the Internet is an easy way to get credit reports quickly. You can go to one of the three major credit bureaus to order, or you can join a service where you pay an annual fee and then a small cost each time you request a report.

Instead of ordering the report over the phone or by mail and then waiting seven to 10 days to see the results, you can order a report online and print it out instantly.

Another Way to Communicate

In the past, communication happened in person, by mail, or by phone. The Internet has created a fourth way known as e-mail.

Recent surveys show that, as of February 2006, 74 percent of homes in the United States have the Internet. Most of these have at least one e-mail address, so you can use the Internet to send e-mails to your tenants. These e-mails can be about routine inspections, new services like garbage disposal, friendly reminders, building newsletters, or even personal messages wishing the tenant a happy birthday.

Although you will need to mail formal notices to your tenants, you can also send them by e-mail. E-mail will allow tenants to view notices more quickly, and it will give you another record showing the date that you contacted them.

The computer can help you keep your information in order, which is a good thing come tax time. In Chapter 13, you will learn about taxes related to real estate investing and how you can ease your tax burden.

13

THE TAX MAN COMETH

THE PURPOSE OF THE TAX MAN

The purpose of the IRS is to tax net income. Net income is money you made minus money you spent to make that money. It sounds simple, but it is far from being so. There are more than 500,000 pages of income tax law text that you have to know to be sure you are doing your taxes correctly. That is why it is so imperative to have an accountant who is knowledgeable about the laws that govern real estate investing as part of your team.

That said, knowing what your accountant will need from you and understanding the basics of tax law will help you run a better business.

The first part of taxable income is gross income — or how much you make. In the real estate investing business, rent is gross income.

There are exceptions to this idea of income, including the following:

- **Loans:** If you receive a loan, that amount loaned to you is not taxable. The IRS makes the distinction as to whether there is a defined time for repayment and interest charged.

- **Gifts:** A gift or inheritance is not considered your income and is not taxable, but the person who gave you the gift may be taxed.

- **Leasehold improvements:** If a tenant makes changes to the property using their own funds, the value of that improvement is not taxable as income.

Now that you know what is excluded from income, let us look at what is included.

Rental Income

Any money you receive due to rent is taxable in the year it was collected. This technicality is particularly important for January rents paid in December, or collections that were due in November but were not collected until February.

This rule also applies to the collection of first and last month's rent. If you collect $1,000 in first and last month's rent in November of 2007, you will owe taxes on that amount in the year 2007. When the tenant moves out, in say 2009, you will use their last month's rent deposit but will NOT have to claim it as income because you already did so back in 2007 when you collected it.

Tenant-Paid Expenses

Ideally, you will never have to deal with emergencies while you are gone, but it can happen. If a tenant pays for a repair, that payment is income.

Trade for Services

If you are lucky and get a handy tenant, they may offer you their services in exchange for the rent or some portion of the rent. If you accept, you are going to have to include a fair market value of the services they rendered as income. For instance, if you have a tenant who lays carpeting and is willing to re-carpet a unit for you in exchange for his $650 rent, you will have to list $650 as income even though you never received any money.

Security Deposits

Unlike first and last month's rent, security deposits are not taxable while you hold onto them. The portion used at the end of the lease will be considered taxable income. For example, if you collect a $1,000 security deposit and use $800 of it to fix up the unit after the tenant leaves, you will only be returning $200 to the tenant. The $800 that you used must be declared as income.

Repairs Versus Improvements

Many landlords incorrectly assume that anything they do on their property is going to be tax deductible. The IRS makes a distinction between repairs and improvement.

Repairs are things that keep your property in good condition. These things include painting, fixing an appliance, and replacing a light fixture. These are deductions (see next section).

On the other hand, improvements to the property add value to the property and are considered income. You cannot deduct expenses, but you can recover your cost by taking depreciation. Improvements include such things as a new roof, new appliances, a deck addition, or the addition of a swimming pool.

Investor Insight: To increase your cash flow, it is better to fix problems quickly and be able to deduct the price rather than wait until problems are so large that they require renovations and can only be recouped over a period of years.

REDUCE THAT INCOME

In most cases, people strive to increase their income. At tax time, however, people are striving to reduce that income, at least on paper. As a real estate investor, you should be no exception.

The second half of the IRS taxing formula of "income - expenses = taxable net income" is the expenses, also known as deductions.

Deductions come about when you spend money on your business, reducing your gross income. Unfortunately, not everything you spend on your business is deductible.

If you spend $500 in postage for your business, that is 100 percent deductible. Spending the same $500 on business meals is only 50 percent deductible. Finally, spending the same amount of money contributing to a political fund that will help reduce property taxes is not deductible.

Rental income provides tax benefits that are greater than most other investments. These benefits will help you realize a profit on your property, but only if you take advantage of them.

Some deductions you will want to take include the following:

Interest: Many forms of interest are deductible if you are a landlord. These include interest from mortgage loans, interest from improvement loans, and credit card interest for goods and services used in your rental business.

Investor Insight: To take the interest of a credit card off as a deduction, you will want to have a credit card used exclusively for goods and services of your properties.

Depreciation: You do not take the actual cost of real estate as a deductible in the first year you buy it. Instead, it is paid for over a specified number of years and is called depreciation. Depreciation will be explained further, later in the chapter.

Repairs: Repairs for what the IRS calls "ordinary, necessary, and reasonable in amount" are deductible in the year that they were sustained. Repairs include re-painting, fixing floors, fixing gutters, fixing the roof (but not complete re-roofing), replacing broken windows, repairing appliances, fixing holes in the walls, or fixing leaks.

Travel: As a landlord, you are entitled to a deduction when you travel for any business related purpose. This travel includes going to your rental unit to talk with a tenant, going to the hardware store to buy a can of paint, or going to the attorney's office to have him check a lease.

You have two different ways to deduct travel expenses. You can deduct actual expenses or use a standard mileage rate. If you use actual expenses, you will need to keep accurate records of gasoline, upkeep, and repairs. To use the standard mileage rate, you must use it the first year you use your car for your business and you must not be deducting an accelerated depreciation on the vehicle.

If you travel long distance for your rental business, you can deduct your airfare, hotel bills, meals, and other trip expenses.

Home Office: You may deduct home office expenses from your income as long as you meet certain requirements. To qualify, you must regularly use a part of your home exclusively for your business and you must either use your home as your principal place of business, meet tenants at your home, or have a detached building you are using as an office on your property. You will be asked for the square footage of space allocated to your business and then you will use form 8829 to figure the tax deductions allowable. By having a home office, you will be able to deduct a portion of your mortgage, utilities, taxes, and repairs on your home.

Employees and Independent Contractors: Any wages you pay can be deducted as a rental expense, especially if you are the true employer and are in charge of giving the employee a W-2, or if they are an independent contractor such as an exterminator.

Casualty and Theft Losses: If you have any damages due to fire or flood, you may be able to take a deduction for your loss or at least a portion of your loss. These types of losses are called casualty losses. The same holds true for theft loss. How much you can deduct depends on how much of your property was destroyed or stolen and whether you had insurance to cover the loss.

Insurance: Insurance payments are deductible for fire, theft, flood, and landlord liability insurance. If you have employees with health insurance and workers' compensation insurance, you can deduct the cost of these as well.

Legal and Professional Services: Any fees paid to your attorney or professionals such as property management companies, real estate investment advisors, or accountants are deductible as long as the work they performed for you was related to your rental activity.

Advertising: The cost of advertisements to find tenants or to find professional help are deductible.

Property Taxes: Landlords may deduct property taxes, and local taxes associated with street maintenance, sidewalks, sewer, or other community services.

Local Services: You can deduct the price of running water and trash collection if you provide them for your tenants.

Rental Items: If you rent furniture for the benefit of a tenant, you can deduct this cost. The cost of renting equipment like steam cleaners or pressure washers is also deductible.

Utilities: Any utilities such as heat, gas, or electric provided to your tenants are deductible.

Tax Preparation: It is wise to deduct the fees of your tax accountant. With all the laws and rules and exceptions associated with tax laws, having someone knowledgeable is worth the price.

IT IS A "LOSS" CAUSE

Finally, you now know your income and know your deductions. It is time to figure your net income. If you subtract your expenses from your gross income and end up with a positive number, you have made a profit, and that profit will be taxed by the IRS. But if you subtract your expenses from your gross income and you end up with a negative number, you are operating at a loss — this is called net operating loss (NOL).

Investor Insight: You can use your NOL against your income in another year or years. If you have a loss of $15,000 in year one, a profit in year two of $2,000, and a profit in year three of $13,000, you can use the loss from year one and use $2,000 of it in year two and the remaining $13,000 in year three.

Net losses still have IRS rules. The IRS differentiates between passive and active participation. If you have passive participation, you may not claim a loss on your business. For instance, if you are an out-of-town landlord who is not directly related to any day-to-day decisions in the business, you will not be able to take the deduction unless it is against a passive gain.

To be an active participant, you need to be involved in at least some of the following:

- Interviewing tenants

- Selecting tenants

- Dealing with tenant issues

- Repairs or maintenance

- Hiring out repair or maintenance work

- Supervising someone you hire

- Deciding which properties to buy

- Deciding which properties to sell

- Determining the rent to charge

In addition to being an active participant, you also have to show the IRS that you are a material participant, meaning that you own at least 10 percent of the property. If you only own 5 percent of the property with other people, you cannot claim the net loss.

Even if you hire a management company, you may qualify as an active participant. For instance, if you continue to approve tenants, set rent levels, and engage in the buying and/or selling of properties, you will be considered active.

Investor Insight: Talk with your CPA to be sure that the duties you perform will classify you as being an active participant for IRS purposes.

The second rule pertaining to net loss is deduction limitations. You are not allowed to deduct more than $25,000 per year as a net loss no matter how many properties you own. The number is even smaller when your income is more than $100,000.

If you have a net loss greater than $25,000, you can use it in subsequent years. You can also use any unused portion to reduce your capital gains when you sell the property.

Even though you have an overall net loss, you need to keep track of which properties had which percentage of the loss so that you can use the right amount of unused loss for capital gains. This loss is easy to track for many expenses like the following:

- Mortgage interest
- Property taxes
- Insurance
- Repairs
- Utilities

Some expenses are not unique to a property but are part of your overall business. For instance:

- Professional fees
- Office supplies
- Automobile expenses
- CPA fees

There are two ways to divide the common expenses: divide evenly among properties or assign them a percentage of rent versus overall rent income.

For example, if you have three properties and $3,000 worth of common expenses, you could just split the amount in three, meaning that $1,000 of the common expenses would be allocated to each property.

Or you can look at the rents of each property. In this example, Property A has a $1,000 rent. Property B has an $850 rent. Property C has a $1,250 rent. When added together, your rental income is $3,100. You can determine the percentage of each of the by dividing the reach rent by the total rent.

Property A is $1,000 / $3,100 = 33 percent

Property B is $850 / $3,100 = 27 percent

Property C is $1,250 / $3,100 = 40 percent

So, give 33 percent of $3,100 to Property A ($990), 27 percent to Property B ($810), and 40 percent to Property C ($1,200).

No matter which way you choose to allocate the funds, keep complete records of what you did and continue to allocate in the same way in future periods.

The last major rule that affects taking a net loss is your Adjusted Gross Income (AGI). If your AGI is higher than $100,000, you have to reduce the amount you can take as a net loss. For each dollar you are over the $100,000 mark, you reduce your net loss deduction by $0.50.

For example, if you have an AGI of $102,000, you have $2,000 more than the allowable amount of income. You have to reduce your net loss by half of the overage, or $1,000. Your maximum net loss would only be $24,000.

Therefore, if your AGI is more than $150,000, you will not be able to claim any rental income losses. Instead, they have to be carried forward and used in years you do not have a high AGI or when you sell the property.

You can determine your AGI by looking on the line items of your IRS 1040 form, but when calculating your AGI for real estate deductions, things are not quite as simple. The modified AGI needed for real estate investment purposes does not allow most of the typical adjustments used to get the AGI.

TWO, FOUR, SIX, EIGHT, WHAT DO WE DEPRECIATE

The next area of tax law you need to understand is depreciation. Depreciation means that you spread your expenses out over the useful life of the purchase rather than take the full deduction the year it was purchased. Depreciation is used on any property that has a useful life longer than one year. Property that meets this criterion is called a capital asset.

Assets such as these are computers, cars, tractors, and houses.

Useful life is when the asset has zero value. For instance, a car after a certain number of years has no book value (financial value).

With houses, however, useful life does not necessarily mean that, at the end of the depreciation period, the house will have no value. As long as you keep up the maintenance and repairs, the home is likely to appreciate in value. Depreciation is used as a way to deduct the asset a little at a time over a prescribed number of years.

Most assets are depreciated using the Modified Cost Recovery System (MACRS). Some assets can be written off using an accelerated rate and others, like real estate, have to use a straight line method.

The recovery period is the time the IRS states the useful life of the asset is. For most real estate investing businesses, your assets will fall into the 5, 7, 27.5, and 31.5 classifications.

> 5 = Autos and trucks, office machinery, computers, landscaping equipment, appliances

> 7 = Office furniture

> 27.5 = Residential real estate (80 percent of the building is used for residential units)

> 31.5 = Nonresidential real estate

With the depreciation tax rules comes the ability to make certain elections, or decisions to use different methods of calculation. After you have chosen which one you are going to use, you have to continue with that method.

You can take your deductions over a longer time than is specified in the rules, which makes sense if your deductions are going to exceed the allowable limit. This strategy will, however, make your taxes even more complicated.

The amount of depreciation you claim in the first year you buy an asset depends on two things:

1. The type of asset involved

2. When you acquired the asset

The mid-month convention calculates your deduction for residential real estate. The half-year deduction applies to most of the other assets you own.

You will be allowed a percentage of depreciation based on the portion of year remaining after the purchase. Each year is broken up into 24 mid-months. So, if you bought a piece of property the first of March for $100,000, you would have 19 mid-months left, or 19/24ths of the year.

Then, to determine how much you would pay for depreciation in the first year, you need to know this number and the number of years the asset will appreciate, which is 27.5 years on residential real estate. Here is how it would work:

19 divided by 24 = .79167

Divide this mid-month number by the depreciation years: .79167 divided by 27.5 = 2.879 percent.

Multiply the percent times the amount the building is worth: 2.879 percent times $100,000 = $2,879.

Instead of determining the percentage yourself, you can also find the percentages listed as a chart available in the Appendix. You can get more specific instructions by going to the IRS Web site, **www.irs.us-treas.gov**, and printing the instructions for form 4562.

Other property is allowed to take accelerated depreciation over a five or seven year period. Accelerated deprecation can either be at 150 or 200 percent.

For these asset classes, the half year convention is used, meaning that the calculation assumes that the asset was placed in service in the middle of the year.

To find out the depreciation of an asset, you would divide the asset value by the number of years of depreciation (5 or 7), and then multiply that by the percentage supplied by the IRS table in form 4562.

There is one big advantage to using acceleration — doing so produces a higher deduction in the early years, which can be helpful with cash flow. However, if you have already exceeded your net loss deduction, then you may wish to have it done in a straight line like your real estate.

There is one more thing to understand about depreciation. You cannot claim depreciation for land — only for improvements on the land. To find out the cost of the improvements on the land, you can do one of three things:

1. Look at the assessed value of your property for tax purposes. This document will list the amount for property and the amount for improvements.

2. Look at an appraisal report. This document will show the current value of buildings and land.

3. Talk to your insurance agent. They identify the value of your improvements because they do not insure the land.

There is no one right way to depreciate your property. It all depends on what you are trying to achieve with your real estate investing business.

It is worth saying one more time — talk with your accountant.

THE 1031 EXCHANGE

Sometimes it is not possible to deduct enough income to keep your taxes at bay. Another thing you can do, besides reduce your tax liability, is to defer your taxes, or move them to a later year.

One such strategy in real estate is going through a 1031 exchange (or like kind) exchange. In a 1031 exchange, you trade one or more properties for one or more replacement properties of like kind, while deferring the payment of federal income taxes and some state taxes on the transaction.

The reason behind a Section 1031 is that, if you own a property but reinvest the money immediately into another property, you did not get any economic gain — at least not the kind you could use to pay taxes. This situation is known as a paper gain — numbers on paper show a gain, but the money in the wallet is not there.

When you do a like kind exchange, you have the same amount of investment, but the form of the investment has changed. For instance, you had two rental homes and now you have a duplex and a rental home, or you had three condos and now you have a six-unit apartment building.

Many people assume that this kind of tax deferral is used for large corporations or professional investors. The truth is that anyone can take advantage of this kind of exchange. You just need to carefully follow the IRS rules in the Internal Revenue Code Section 1031.

Here is a quick summary of the rules:

1. The original and the replacement property must be for investment purposes. If you plan to flip the property, it will not qualify for a 1031, nor will your personal residence.

2. The original and replacement properties must be like kind. All qualifying real property located in the United States is like kind. Property located outside the United States is not like kind to property located in the United States.

3. The whole process has to be finished within 180 days of the sale of the original property.

4. The price of the replacement property has to be higher than the sales price of the original property.

5. Funds must go through a third party.

6. The seller of the replacement property has to sign stating that they agree to the like kind exchange.

There are five different types of 1031 exchange. The simultaneous exchange happens when the original property and the replacement property are exchanged at the same time.

A delayed exchange is the most common type of 1031 exchange. Delayed exchange occurs when there is a time between the transfer of the original property and the gaining of the replacement property. This type of exchange has strict time limits.

The build-to-suit exchange concerns improvements or constructions, and it allows you to build on or improve the replacement property using the proceeds from the exchange.

A reverse exchange is when the replacement property is acquired while you have the original property. These are sometimes known as "parking arrangements." As with the delayed exchange, the amount of time that you can have both properties in your possession is limited.

Finally, there is the personal property exchange where you can exchange personal property, real estate, or other assets for like kind or like class, but you cannot exchange different classes like diamond rings for property.

The 1031 exchange merely defers taxes. When you finally sell the property in a way that it is not part of an exchange, you will have to pay the taxes on the original deterred gain plus any new gain since the purchase of the replacement property. You can find out more rules by going to **www.irs.com** and downloading form 8824 and publication 544.

KEEPING THE RECORDS

Keeping records is a must if you want to take all the deductions available to you as a real estate investor. Without the records, you have no proof and that leads to some big problems where the IRS is concerned.

Investor Insight: If you document each item as it occurs, you will be less likely to forget the information or lose the receipts.

For each expense you need to know the following:

- The amount of the expense

- What the expense covers (categorized by IRS deductions)

- Who received the payment

- The date the expense was incurred

- The date the expense was paid

There are some items you should file so that you can prove your expenses were warranted, allowed, and true. These receipts and other items will help you during tax time and help in case of an audit.

Here are just a few items you should keep on file:

1. **As a landlord, you will need to keep copies of all tenant information**, all vacancies, and all the advertisements you place

to find new tenants. You will need to show proof that you intend to use the property as an investment over the long term. If you can show long-term leases, a low vacancy rate, and/or advertisements that show that you are seeking tenants, you will have proof that you are using the property as a rental and not just renting it until you sell it.

2. **Keep the receipts** — all of them. To verify your expenses with the IRS, you will have to have receipts or canceled checks. Instead of shoving everything into a shoebox, you should have an orderly system that allows you to come up with everything you will need. For instance, you can have your receipts filed by category and in each category, have the receipts ordered by date. Keep receipts for insurance paid, service bills from plumbers and electricians, supplies, advertising, and agency fees.

3. **Document all depreciation.** Keep receipts of all improvements and all purchases of equipment. Keep the depreciation you have claimed in previous years as well. When you sell the property, the IRS will have you factor the depreciation to find the true profit of the sale.

4. **Keep a car log.** If you use your car for business related purposes, you can deduct mileage, but only if you keep a detailed, written log. It is best to keep this log in your car. Otherwise, you will forget to write in it. The IRS does not want estimations. They do no want total miles, either. They want the beginning and ending mileage and the purpose and date of the trip. To make your log even more foolproof, log other trips in the car stating the same information but state that it was non-business.

Keeping records separate is imperative. Many real estate investors are part-time investors with other jobs. Small investors often use a home office for their work. It is easy to mix business with home under these situations, but you should be warned that if you do, you will not be happy with the results after an IRS audit.

The biggest thing you can do to separate home and business is to have a separate checking account and credit card for your business. Having a separate account shows the IRS that you are serious about keeping your home and your business separate. It will also help you since your statements will be more written proof about how much you spent, and where and when you spent it.

Even if you keep every receipt and read every book on real estate investing, you are not likely to be able to do your own taxes and get the deductions you deserve. An accountant will help you get deductions, make decisions to help with subsequent years' tax liabilities, and keep you out of trouble.

An accountant can do all of the following for you:

- Create a list of categories for which you can take tax deductions

- Tell you IRS limits on deductions

- Identify the IRS forms you need to submit

- Help you fill out the forms for an in-home office

- Keep repairs and improvements separate

- Advise you on which depreciation methods are best for you

- Help you make decisions about your future income and expenses with tax saving strategies

- Establish long-term goals

- Factor all the depreciation when you sell a property to determine profit

- Keep up with changing tax laws

- Find deductions you did not know existed

- Identify problems early on

- Help with quarterly taxes

- And last, but not lease, prepare accurate tax returns

At tax time, every landlord should use an accountant. If the fee bothers you, consider the alternatives — lost money in depreciation or an audit — and you will see that it is worth it. Best of all, the fee is tax deductible.

NET LOSS GETS EVEN BETTER

Business Entity

If you have not set up an actual company for your investment properties, you may want to consider doing so. The three main ways to set up a business for the purpose of real estate investing are the S corporation, the partnership, and the LLC.

The S corporation is a corporation that has its income taxes directly on shareholder returns. This type of entity will give less your personal liability if someone were to get hurt on your property, but it does not help in terms of taxes.

A partnership, on the other hand, offers tax benefits but does not protect you from personal liability. If someone gets hurt on your property, they can sue you, not just your partnership.

The last type of entity is the limited liability corporation (LLC). The LLC is a combination of the S corporation and the partnership; it offers personal liability protection and the use of good tax benefits. Before deciding on a business entity, talk with your accountant and attorney.

When you have an LLC, no matter what happens to the property held by the LLC, nothing can happen to your own personal assets. That means that, if someone sues because they got hurt on an investment property, they cannot come after your home, your car, your boat, or any other asset. The same is true for creditors of the LLC.

Advantages of an LLC

In terms of taxes, the LLC is far better than a corporation. There are several reasons why.

The first is that an LLC has pass-through treatment, meaning that the LLC is not a taxpayer. It just passes income, gains, losses, expenses, and tax credits to its owners. It is the responsibility of each owner to report his own share of the LLC income and loss on their own personal tax return.

Investor Insight: An LLC does not have to have more than one member. You can own an LLC as the sole owner and get the benefits of having personal liability protection.

If you own the LLC as a sole owner, you will complete a Schedule C stating the income or loss you incurred as a member of the LLC.

If the LLC has multiple owners, it files an LLC partnership return, IRS form 1065. This form states the business activities of the LLC. It also allocates income, deductions, and other items according to ownership interests. Each owner then reports this allocation, or distributive share, on their personal tax return on Schedule E.

For example, assume there are three members of the LLC. Member A owns 50 percent while members B and C own 25 percent each. The LLC would file Form 1065 stating the activities of the LLC and would assign any income, deductions, tax credits, and other items at 50 percent for LLC Member A and at 25 percent for Members B and C. Then all three members do their taxes and report this percentage of income and deductions on their Schedule E.

Investor Insight: State income tax rules for LLCs differ from state to state, but most states follow the federal tax treatment. States get extra money from LLCs by charging an annual fee from $100 to $800.

The biggest advantage to an LLC is that the owner of an LLC can use the net loss of the LLC as a deduction on their personal return, meaning that, if the LLC takes a loss, that loss does not have to be held over, but can be used immediately on your own personal taxes. You can use the LLC loss to offset your own income from other sources, even wages from an employer.

Limits on LLC Owner Net Loss Deductions

The tax law for LLCs does take into account your "basis" and imposes loss limitations based on such. For instance, if you have a rental property that has a net loss of $30,000, but you have a basis of $25,000, you cannot use the entire loss.

A tax basis is the money you put into your LLC. For example, if you put $100,000 into one rental property and $75,000 into another, and you are the sole owner of the LLC, your tax basis would be $175,000. Your basis is increased by loans you make to the LLC and loans used to acquire an asset. So, if you use a mortgage to buy a property, your basis is increased by the amount of the debt.

Continuing the example, if the LLC uses a mortgage of $250,000 to purchase another rental property, your basis would go from $175,000 to $425,000.

Losses are also limited by passive activity loss rules. Rental holdings are considered passive activities. According to the rules, you cannot have passive losses that exceed passive income. In other words, if you only take in $30,000 worth of real estate income, you can only assume that much debt. Anything above that passive amount has to be carried forward or used when you sell off your interest in the LLC. You are able to use losses that are $25,000 more than passive income as long as you do not have an adjusted AGI of $100,000 or more.

Real Estate Professional Status

You can get around the passive loss rules if you are considered a real estate professional. To be a real estate professional, you have to spend a certain number of hours each year in real estate activities.

Internal Revenue Code Section 468 (c) (7) states the definition of a real estate professional. You must work at least 750 hours annually in the real estate business (about 15 hours a week), and you must spend at least half your time actively engaged in the real estate business.

You do not have to meet these requirements as part of an LLC. For example, if you work in the construction business, you spend half your time and the required hours working in a real estate field. If you qualify this way, you will also have to materially participate in the rental activity. That would make you eligible to take passive income losses greater than the passive income of your properties.

To be treated by the IRS as a real estate professional, you must attach that election to your tax return. After they accept that status, it cannot be revoked unless there is a change in your life to indicate it.

More Than One LLC

You should get a separate LLC for each property.

One of the big advantages to an LLC is protection against personal liability. The LLC can, however, be sued. If you have a different LLC for each property, then a problem with one property cannot affect any of the other holdings you have.

If you already own a business and want to buy a piece of property, you can do so with your business entity, but it may not be a wise idea. If you buy the property separate from your business, you will have more flexibility in selling it in the future and you will not have any business liabilities affect the property.

Now that you understand taxes and the benefit of hiring a real estate accountant, you are ready to move on to the final chapter. In Chapter 14, you will learn how to use your real estate holdings as a retirement investment.

14

RENTAL RETIREMENT

For many people, real estate investing is part of a larger plan — a retirement plan. You want to have a comfortable retirement fund. You want to have a steady flow of income on retiring. You want to be able to enjoy life, and you want to know whether it can be done using real estate as the tool.

If done correctly, the answer is yes. Real estate investing can make you a tidy sum.

Real estate investing leaves you many different options. You can decide what you wish to invest in, and you can determine how those investments will work for you when you retire. Some of your options are as follows:

1. You could sell all your holdings and use that money as your nest egg.

2. You could keep all your holdings and use the rent coming in as your monthly cash flow to pay your expenses.

3. You could cash some of your holdings in and keep some earning income.

The only thing you have to decide is what mix is right for you. If you decide to keep the properties as rentals after you retire, you can keep the money flowing in. You may choose to have someone else manage the properties, which will cut into your cash flow a bit, but depending on the number of properties you own and your cash flow needs, this may be a good solution for you.

If you choose to buy, rent, and then sell before retirement, you can use that money in a way that can create residual income for you by investing in vehicles that give you a monthly return.

Real estate investing has its pros and cons, just like any other investment vehicle. As a real estate investor, you will get to enjoy tax benefits and see your properties rise in value. You will be able to use other people's money to build up your own. Also, however, you will have to worry about negative cash flows, slow markets, unruly tenants, and an investment that needs time to become liquid — you cannot sell a house as quickly as you can sell a stock.

For many people, the advantages outweigh the disadvantages, and real estate investing becomes part of a retirement plan portfolio.

Been There, Done That

Aziz Abdur-Ra'oof gives us this real life example:

"I have a friend who found out about a co-op in the same neighborhood with the United Nations. The co-op was 300 square feet and was selling for $100,000. That is not a misprint. Trust me, this is prime real estate.

"She financed $79,200, and since she had at least 20 percent down, she did not have to have personal mortgage insurance (PMI). The debt service costs her $6,403 per year. During her first year, she made $1,107, or 4.5 percent return. During her second year, however, she did not incur any closing costs, so she had $5,683, or 22.9 percent return. As the years went along, the rental prices increased somewhat and she went from a 25.3 percent return in year three to a 30.6 percent return in year five. Her five-year pretax average return was 22.2 percent."

If you had one of these deals each year for the next 10 years, you would make $7,500 cash flow per year per deal. That means that, after the last deal, you would have a positive cash flow of $75,000. Now, let us assume that you do not wish to be the one who maintains these ten properties. You can hire a general repairman for $30,000 and make $45,000 with no hassles.

RULE OF 72

There is an investing rule that lets you see how quickly your funds will double over time. It is called the Rule of 72. To find out how long it will take for your money to double, you divide 72 by the annual percentage rate you are receiving on a sum of money.

For example, if you have a property making an 8 percent ROI, you can expect your investment to double in nine years (72 divided by 8). That means that, if you invested $5,000 on a $100,000 property, nine years later that principal will have doubled to $10,000. But in real estate, that only accounts for the ROI that you are receiving in rent. Add to that the appreciation you will receive on the property in a nine year period and you will see an even larger increase.

Since 1968, houses averaged an appreciation rate of 6.34 percent a year. So in addition to earning $5,000 in rent income over the nine year period, you will have earned 6.34 percent for nine years and gained an appreciation value of nearly $35,000.

Imagine repeating this scenario with several different properties, each with $5,000 invested, and you can see how high the earnings can be.

Cash Flow or Appreciation Profits — You Decide

Before getting started in investing too quickly, you need to think about how you plan to use the properties. Do you want to buy and hold or do you plan to buy and sell? Either answer is acceptable, but different answers will require that you make different decisions when you buy your properties — decisions in what you will buy and how much you will spend.

Mistakes can easily be made if you are buying for one market, but making decisions based on another.

Looking at the buy and sell market, you will want to know the cost of repairs so that you can see if a home is being sold far enough below value for you to buy it, fix it up, rent it for a year or two, and then sell it. You will need to understand the difference between repairs that will provide good returns quickly and those that will not. In some markets, adding granite countertops is a good way to increase the value of a home; in other markets, you would just be wasting your time.

There are other improvements that almost never add enough in additional value to even cover the expense. Adding a swimming pool is one of them.

If you plan to buy and sell, you need to buy properties that can be sold quickly and at a profit. When you are buying and then selling in a short time (under five years) you want to try to minimize your interest expense. Buying a property with a short-term holding plan that cannot increase in value quickly in five years and has a large interest rate loan will not be a good choice.

If you are holding property for the long-term, you need to understand long-term numbers. How much can the property support in rent? How much will the mortgage payments be? How many other expenses will the property incur? If you are buying to hold, buying a property with a negative cash flow makes no sense.

One of the biggest mistakes you can make is to assume that appreciation on the house will outpace the negative cash flow. It may not happen. Not to mention that you are losing money in the meantime. With houses that you intend to buy and keep, you want to have a positive cash flow as well as appreciation. If you start negative on the first count, you will never make as much positive on the second count no matter what the market does.

When you hold a property for the long term, you expect to earn profits immediately — just as soon as you can get a tenant situated in your unit. The ideal situation is that you achieve a positive cash flow, but due to depreciation and deductions have a net loss. This way, you can enjoy the profits without having to pay the taxes.

MAKE THE APPRAISER YOUR FRIEND

When you plan to sell properties, either right away or in the future, you need to think about market value. Market value is the amount someone will truly pay for your house, and it can be affected by the following:

- Architecture

- Landscaping

- Neighborhood

- Convenience

- Other properties in the area

If someone wishes to purchase your property as a rental unit, other things that will affect the price include the following:

- Number of rental units

- Amount of rent tenants are willing to pay

- Likelihood that rents will go up

In the best of circumstances, the market value will increase by the time you are ready to sell simply because that is what property has historically done.

You can add to that increase through improvements. You can make the house have a higher market value by doing the following:

- Building an addition
- Replacing a roof
- Putting up a fence
- Adding a deck
- Paving a driveway
- Adding landscaping

There is no guarantee that such improvements will positively increase the market value of your home, but by observing other homes in the area, and the price of home sales in your area, you can make determinations about what will make your property have a higher market value and what will not.

One way to determine whether an improvement will increase the market value of your home is to think like an appraiser. What does the appraiser look for when he comes into your home and determines its price? Some things are beyond your control. For instance, you cannot change what the market is doing in your neighborhood, nor can you change the location of your property; but there are things he will look at that you do have control over, such as:

- Windows
- Screens
- Heating and cooling systems
- Insulation
- Kitchen appliances
- Garages
- Materials used, such as granite, compared with the rest of the neighborhood

Another way to determine what improvements will make the market value increase is to compare your home to the other homes. If all the homes in the neighborhood have skylights and large decks, adding one to your home will likely increase the market value of the home. On the other hand, if no one in the neighborhood has either, you are not likely to get buyers to purchase your house for more just because it does have those features.

Finally, you need to be aware of factors that are beyond your control. Such things can be supply and demand in your area, the economic health of the region, or even a new transit system that bypasses your neighborhood. Knowing about these factors can help you decide whether adding improvements will get someone to buy. If the economic health in the area is down and people are moving away to find work, no amount of improvements in your home will get them to stay.

In addition to thinking strictly of how you will use your investment properties to purchase your retirement, you can also think about how you can use current retirement fund monies to purchase real estate. A self-directed real estate IRA is the answer.

IRA YOUR WAY

Traditional IRAs do not allow you to make key decisions concerning the investments of the money. You make the determination to have the money in this fund or that one, but then you are left out of the loop until it is statement time.

A self-directed IRA gives you the chance to invest in ways that are not so traditional. It allows you to invest in an asset you know and understand — real estate.

With a fully self-directed IRA, you make all your own investment selections. Since you plan to invest in real estate, it is essential that you find a plan administrator that has administered an IRA with such investments. To find such an administrator, you can do an Internet Search.

There are no restrictions on the type of real estate investments you can use as an IRA investment. Such investments include not only houses, but apartment complexes, hotels and motels, and office buildings. A self-directed IRA allows you to invest your retirement funds into an investment that is tangible while giving you the ability to control and understand your investments.

Financial experts will tell you to avoid real estate holdings through your IRA because such investments are too difficult. The truth is, that there are IRS rules and codes that you will need to be aware of, but hiring a good tax accountant and plan administrator will make the investments problem-free.

When using your IRA, you can form an LLC, a partnership, or even pool resources. All of these strategies are within the law and make investing through your IRA as easy as investing any other way.

Some of the tax benefits of real estate investing are lost, however, to IRA real estate investing. For instance, you cannot write off depreciation since you are getting your tax break by putting the property into a tax exempt entity.

MAKING IT SELF DIRECTED

When you choose to establish a self-directed IRA, you can do so by means of a traditional or Roth IRA. All self-directed IRAs have a trustee called an IRA custodian, an IRA administrator, or an IRA advisor. These trustees charge a setup fee and annual fees for their efforts.

Fees are quite different across different companies. The initial fee can be no more than $50 or as high as $2,000. Then there are annual fees that range from $200 and up. Fees are so different because each trustee can do different things for you. The more they do, the more they will charge you.

IRA custodians merely hold your money for you and put it where you tell them to. They have the least expensive fees because they do the least.

IRA advisors do what custodians do and help you find properties, do all the paperwork, help you with legal documents, and much more. Their fees are significantly higher than that of a custodian.

Before determining which custodian, administrator, or advisor to use, check with the Better Business Bureau and your state's Attorney General's office. If you have friends using a self-directed IRA, see who they recommend. After you have narrowed it down to three or four choices, take all the initial paperwork to your attorney and have him look it over and explain anything that may be confusing to you.

While any form of IRA allows for real estate investment, there are other pros and cons to consider when choosing the account type best for you.

- A **traditional IRA** lets you deduct annual contributions from your income, but when you begin withdrawing money, those funds will be taxed as regular income.

- A **Roth IRA** gives you no deduction on your current contributions, but does allow you to withdraw funds tax free. If you expect to buy a real estate investment in an IRA and hold it for a long period, this is most likely your best option, particularly if the property increases in value over that period.

- A **SEP-IRA** is designed for self-employed individuals and small companies. This option is a good alternative for real estate investors who can make the higher contributions because they can build up funds more rapidly to purchase properties.

KEEPING YOUR ACCOUNT TAX DEFERRED

Once you have created a self-directed IRA with an administrator that allows real estate holders, you will be able to start investing. However, it is necessary to talk with a retirement planning accountant so that your IRA will maintain its tax-deferred status.

Mistakes are easily made if you do not know the IRS rules. Even unintentional mistakes can get your IRA account into big trouble leading to taxes and penalties that surpass the price of your real estate investments.

Here are three rules that will help keep your investments tax deferred:

1. Every transaction must go through your IRA. Transactions through a personal account make your investment taxable. Even if you only make a small transaction through a personal account, your entire investment will lose the tax-free status.

2. The title for the investment needs to be in the IRA trustee name or the company that holds your IRA and not your own. Placing the title in your own name will keep you from transferring the property to your IRA.

3. All profits must go directly into your IRA account. You are allowed to reinvest your earnings, but only through your IRA. If you take out the profits, even a small portion of the profits, your entire investment will no longer be part of your IRA creating early withdrawal and penalty fees.

DO WHAT THE IRS SAYS

There are many rules governing the use of IRA funds. Such rules include, but are not limited to, the following:

- Properties held in your IRA cannot be your own residence. For instance, you could buy a retirement home, rent it to someone else, put the rental income in your IRA, and, when you retire, take the house as a distribution. Then you can move in.

- They cannot be purchased from your immediate family, but can be purchased from your siblings.

- You may not own the property purchased by your plan. It has to be owned by your IRA.

- You must ensure that your intended purchase is not a prohibited transaction. A prohibited transaction involves the improper use of your IRA holdings by you or any disqualified person. A disqualified person is any member of your immediate family (except siblings), employers, certain partners, fiduciaries, and other categories specified in the IRS code. Find a good advisor because IRS laws can be tricky.

- It must be for investment purposes only.

- Your business may not lease or be located in or on any part of the property while it is in your plan.

Investor Insight: Using your IRA for real estate purposes can be tricky due to IRS laws. Because the laws governing IRA transactions are so complicated, you should consult with an experienced real estate professional.

CONCLUSION

Real estate is an excellent tool for building wealth, and rental properties are one way to do so.

No investment is perfect. Dealing with tenants, trying to figure out the tax laws, and dealing with repairs and maintenance can be a headache. It is up to you to determine whether the advantages outweigh the disadvantages.

Real estate investing is not a get rich quick scheme. You must do your homework, be involved, and have a long-term investment plan to realize the most profit from the endeavor. Nonetheless, if you stick with it, you will realize high profits and be able to use that money to reach your financial goals.

This book contains the information you need to make an informed choice. You should realize by now that this is a business. If you are not committed to the process, you will not succeed.

If you do follow the plan outlined in this book, you have a good chance of making real estate investing work for you. You have the knowledge to begin investing in real estate. You understand what it will take. You are ready to buy your first property.

Happy investing.

APPENDIX

RENTAL APPLICATION

Date: _____

Application is hereby made to rent premises described as _____ for a term of _____ and ending the _____ day of _____, 20___, for which monthly rental shall be _____, payable in advance, and for which a security deposit of $ _____ shall be due before occupancy of the above-described premises.

A deposit of _____ is made herewith on account of the first month's rent, with the understanding that if this application is accepted and the applicant fails to execute a lease before the beginning date specified above, or to pay the balance due as first month's rent, said payment will be forfeited as liquidated damages. It is also understood that if this application is not accepted, or if the premises are not ready for occupancy by the applicant on the date specified above, said deposit shall be refunded to the applicant forthwith, on applicant's request.

APPLICANT/SPOUSE INFORMATION

Name: _____ SS #: _____

Driver's License #: _____ State: _____

Spouse's Name: _____ SS#:_____

Driver's License #_____ State:_____

Number of children:_____

Number of dogs:_____ Number of cats:_____

Other pets, please state what kind and how many of each: _____
_____

RENTAL APPLICATION

ADDRESS INFORMATION:

Current Address:_____

How long have you been at your current address?_____

If less than 5 years, please give your previous address:_____
_____

How long were you living at the previous address? _____

EMPLOYMENT INFORMATION

Applicant:

Current Employer: _____

Employer Address: _____

Name of person to contact at your employment: _____

Contact Phone Number: _____

Number of years employed? _____

Annual Income: _____

If you have been employed with this company less than 5 years, where was your former employment?_____

Name of person to contact at your former employment:_____

Contact Phone Number of former employment:_____

Spouse:

Current Employer: _____

Employer Address: _____

Name of person to contact at your employment: _____

Contact Phone Number: _____

Number of years employed? _____

Annual Income: _____

If you have been employed with this company less than 5 years, where was your former employment?_____

RENTAL APPLICATION

Name of person to contact at your former employment:_____

Contact Phone Number of former employment:_____

REFERENCES

Employer Reference:_____ Phone:_____

Personal Reference: _____Phone:_____

Credit Reference:_____ Phone:_____

The information provided herein may be used by the landlord or his agent to determine whether to accept this application. On written request within____ days, the landlord or his agent will disclose to applicant in writing the nature and scope of any investigation landlord has requested, and will, if this application is refused, state in writing the reason for said refusal.

Accepted _____ Denied_____

APPLICANT DENIAL LETTER

Date: _____

Dear Applicant,

The application you placed for rental of the premises described as _____ located at _____ (street), _____ (city), ____ (state) _____ (zip) has unfortunately been denied.

The reason for our denial of your rental application was:

☐ Application contained incomplete or false information or the information that you provided on your application could not be verified.

☐ Previous rental history was reported as unfavorable for applicant.

☐ Did not meet income or debt-to-income qualifications.

☐ Information contained in your credit report.

In accordance with the Fair Credit Reporting Act, we are required to inform you where credit information was gathered from. We obtained this report from:

☐ Experian (TRW) Consumer Assistance, P.O. Box 949, Allen, TX 75002, 800-682-7654

APPLICANT DENIAL LETTER

☐ Trans Union Consumer Relations, P.O. Box 1000, 2 Baldwin Place, Chester, PA 19022, 800-888-4213

☐ CBI/Equifax Credit Information Service, P.O. Box 740241, Atlanta, GA 30374-2041, 800-685-1111

Insufficient credit information was obtained from the credit reporting agency marked above.

The credit reporting agency marked above was unable to provide a sufficient amount of information about you.

A person or company provided background information about you. Within 60 days of receiving this letter, you have the right to request information on the nature of the information provided. You must make this request in writing. Under federal law, we are prohibited from releasing information regarding the source of this information.

The credit reporting agency marked above may have gathered credit information on you based on reports from one of the other agencies. The agencies above serve only to provide credit information and were in no manner directly responsible for the denial of your rental application.

Under federal law, you have the right to receive a copy of your credit report, to dispute the accuracy and completeness of the report, and to insert a statement regarding specific entries on your credit report. Call the credit reporting agency marked above if you believe that there is inaccurate information contained on your credit report. You can also write the credit reporting agency at the address listed above to inform them of inaccuracies. A disclosure of the inaccuracies can be made orally, in writing, or electronically. Contact the agency marked above for specific details of on filing complaints.

Within 60 days of ____/____/____, you are eligible to receive a free copy of your consumer credit report from the agency marked above.

You may have additional rights under the credit reporting or consumer protection laws of your state. If you wish, you may contact your state or local consumer protection agency or a state Attorney General's office.

Best Regards,

_____

Landlord/Property Manager

APPLICANT DISCLOSURE FORM

I hereby request that my application for the following rental property (address) _____be reviewed by _____.

Applicant Name:_____

Applicant Social Security Number:_____

Date of Birth:_____

Driver's License:_____ State:_____

Applicant Address:_____

_____

Applicant Home Phone:_____

Applicant Cell Phone:_____

Applicant Work Phone:_____

Address of Rental:_____

_____

I give my authorization for _____to obtain and review my consumer credit report and any public records needed to come to an applicant decision. I also authorize _____ to investigate any other personal information for the same purpose.

Signature_____

Date_____/_____/_____

WEEK-TO-WEEK RENTAL CONTRACT

This week-to-week rental contract is entered into on this date, _____, 20__ by and between _____(Owner) and _____(Renter).

WITNESSETH: That for and in consideration of the payment of the rent due and the performance of the covenants contained on the part of the Renter, said Owner does hereby demise and let unto the Renter, and Renter hires from Owner for use as a residence the specific premises hereby described as _____ which are located at _____ (street), _____ (city), ___ (state) _____ (zip) for a tenancy from week-to-week beginning on _____ (date) until _____ (ending date) at a weekly price of _____ dollars, for a total rental amount of _____(dollars), payable in advance on the first day of tenancy.

The following are also mutually agreed upon by both Renter and Owner:

WEEK-TO-WEEK RENTAL CONTRACT

1. Renter shall not violate any city ordinance or state law in or about the rental location.

2. Renter shall not sub-let the rental property, or any part thereof, or assign this contract without the written consent of said Owner.

3. Renter shall give immediate notice to the Owner or agent of same should any fire, theft, or vandalism occur on said premises.

4. Renter must not make any alterations or improvements to said property unless prior written consent has been given by Owner.

5. If legal action takes place or must be initiated by Owner, Renter agrees to pay all costs, expenses, as well as all attorney's fees, as the court may affix.

Arrival Date: _____ Arrival Time: _____(__p.m./__a.m.)

Departure Date: _____ Departure Time: _____(__p.m./__a.m.)

Said premises ___are / ___are not furnished with furniture, cooking utensils, kitchen equipment, linens, and bedding.

The following items are furnished: _____

_____

A non-refundable $_____ deposit is required in order to reserve said premises each week.

A deposit of $_____ for cleaning is required at time of check in. Cleaning deposit will be refunded only if said premises are left in clean condition at the time of check out.

If Owner is to incur any cleaning expenses in order to restore said premises to the condition they were in at the time of Renter's occupancy, the amount required for said restoration will be deducted from the cleaning deposit and any remaining funds from the cleaning deposit will be refunded to the Renter.

_____

Owner Signed

_____

Owner Printed

_____

Renter Signed

_____

Renter Printed

SAMPLE LEASE

Courtesy of Aziz Abdur-Ra'oof of Keller Williams® Realty Centre

LEASE AGREEMENT

This Agreement is made this _____ day of _____, 20_____, and is between _____ _____ (hereinafter referred to as "Landlord") and _____ _____, jointly and severally, (hereinafter referred to as "Resident"). Landlord rents to Resident, and Resident rents from Landlord, property located at:

Address: _____ City: _____,

State: _____ Zip: _____, the full legal description of which is the same recorded with the Clerk of the Superior Court of _____ County, and is made part hereof by reference (hereinafter referred to as the "Property") under the following terms and conditions:

1. **TERM:** The initial term of this Agreement shall be made for _____ months beginning on the_____ day of _____, 20_____, and terminating on the _____ day of _____, 20_____.

2. **POSSESSION:** Should Landlord be unable to deliver possession of the Property at the commencement of this Agreement, Landlord shall not be liable for damages caused thereby, nor shall this Agreement be void or voidable, but the Resident shall not be liable for any rent until possession is delivered. As long as premises is habitable, Resident may not reasonably refuse to occupy.

3. **RENT:** Rent is payable monthly in advance without notice or demand at the rate of _____ DOLLARS ($_____) per month, on the first day of each month during the initial or any extended term of this Agreement, and shall be annually adjusted. For the period _____ to _____, Resident shall pay a pro rated monthly rental of $_____. Unless otherwise notified in writing, the monthly rental payment shall increase annually by ten percent (10 percent) payable monthly beginning the month following the initial term and adjusting annually thereafter. Rental payments shall be mailed to:

_____

_____

_____

4. **ADDITIONAL RENT:** If Landlord elects to accept rent after the 5th day of the month, Resident will pay, as additional rent, a charge of five percent (5 percent) of the monthly rental as a late charge. This payment shall not constitute as a

SAMPLE LEASE
Courtesy of Aziz Abdur-Ra'oof of Keller Williams® Realty Centre

waiver of the Landlord's right to institute proceedings for rent, damages, and/or repossession of the Property for non-payment of any installment of rent.

5. **APPLICATION OF PAYMENTS:** All payments from Resident to Landlord may, at Landlord's option, be applied in the following order to debts owed by Resident to Landlord; late charges, agent's fees, attorney's fees, court costs, obligations other than rent (if any) due to Landlord, other past due rent other than monthly rent, past due monthly rent, current monthly rent.

6. **RETURNED CHECKS:** In the event any check given by Resident to Landlord is returned by the bank unpaid, Resident agrees to pay the Landlord THIRTY-FIVE ($35.00) DOLLARS as additional rent and agrees to pay the five percent (5 percent) monthly late fee. This charge will be waived if the bank verifies, in writing, the check was returned due to their error. Any returned check must be redeemed by cashier's check, certified check, or money order. In the event more than one check is returned, Resident herewith agrees to pay all future rents and charges in the form of cashier's check, certified check, or money order.

7. **SECURITY DEPOSIT:** Landlord herby acknowledges receipt from Resident of the sum of $_____, paid prior hereto, to be held as security for the faithful performance by the Resident of the covenants, conditions, rules and regulations contained herein. The Security Deposit, or any portion thereof, may be withheld for unpaid rent, damage due to breach of this Lease or for damage(s) by Resident or the Resident's family, agents, employees, guests, or invitees in excess of ordinary wear and tear to the Property and major appliances owned by the Landlord. It is understood and agreed, however, that irrespective of said Security Deposit, rent shall be paid when due, in accordance with the terms hereof. The Resident shall have the right to be present when the Landlord, or the Landlord's agent, inspects the Property to determine if any damage was done to the Property, if the Resident notifies the Landlord by certified mail of the Resident's intention to move, the moving date, and the Resident's new address. The notice to be furnished by the Resident shall be mailed fifteen (15) days before the date of moving. On receipt of the notice, the Landlord shall notify the Resident by certified mail of the time and date when the Property is to be inspected. The date of the inspection shall occur within five (5) days before or five (5) days after the date of moving as designated in the Resident's notice.

8. **EARLY TERMINATION:** In the event Resident shall elect to terminate this Lease, or any renewal or extension thereof, before its expiration date, Landlord agrees to permit said early termination on Resident giving Landlord two (2) months written notice of

SAMPLE LEASE

Courtesy of Aziz Abdur-Ra'oof of Keller Williams® Realty Centre

Resident's intent to terminate, with Resident agreeing, in writing, to pay Landlord an amount equal to two (2) additional month's rent beyond the end of the month in which the Resident elects to terminate this Lease. This offer is contingent on Resident being current in the monthly rental at the time Resident vacates, and with the amount equal to two (2) additional month's rent being paid before such termination.

9. **CONDITION:** Resident accepts Property in its present "AS-IS" condition and acknowledges that the Resident has received a list of any existing damages to the Property, been given the right to inspect the same, and has approved said list except as previously specified in writing to Landlord. Resident acknowledges receipt of: "Move-In Inspection Form" and accepts the responsibility to complete said form within seven (7) days of taking possession and return a completed, signed copy to Landlord. Failure to do so shall be Resident's acknowledgement that Property is in perfect condition in every particular and that any damages, including breakage, burns and wear or otherwise not shown shall be Resident's responsibility and expense.

10. **MAINTENANCE REPAIRS:** Landlord shall be responsible for repairs to the Property, its equipment and appliances furnished by Landlord, except that Resident agrees to pay the cost for all labor and material for repairs or replacement if the damage or malfunction to the Property, its equipment or appliances or any other part of the Property, is due to the Resident, Resident's family, employees, agents, guests or invitees. In the event Resident fails to give Landlord prompt notice of the need for repairs, Resident shall be liable to Landlord for any increased cost of repairs arising out of such failure.

11. **ALTERATIONS:** Resident shall not make any alterations, installations, repairs, or redecorations of any kind to the Property without prior written permission of Landlord, provided however, that notwithstanding such consent, Resident agrees that all alterations, including, without limitations, any items affixed to the Property, shall become the property of Landlord on termination of this Agreement. This includes, but is not limited to, ceiling fans, mini blinds, carpeting, fencing, lighting fixtures, shrubs, and flowers. Removal of these items shall be considered theft subject to civil and criminal prosecution.

12. **USE:** The Property shall be used for Residential purposes only and shall be occupied by the undersigned _____ adults and their _____ children as named in the original application to rent, only. Occupancy by guests staying over 14 days will be considered violation of this Agreement. The Property shall be used so as to comply with all state, county, and municipal laws and ordinances and shall be kept in a clean and orderly condition. Resident shall not use the Property

SAMPLE LEASE

Courtesy of Aziz Abdur-Ra'oof of Keller Williams® Realty Centre

or permit it to be used for any disorderly or unlawful purpose or in any manner so as to interfere with neighbors. Resident shall be responsible and fully liable for the conduct of his/her guest. Acts of guest in violation of this Agreement or Landlord's rules and regulations may be deemed by Landlord to be a breach by Resident.

13. **SMOKE DETECTORS:** Landlord has installed at least one smoke detector in the Premises and that said detector(s) is in good condition and proper working order as of the beginning of the Lease term. Resident agrees not to obstruct or tamper with said detector(s) or otherwise permit the detector(s) to be obstructed or tampered with for any reason whatsoever. Resident further agrees to test the detector(s) periodically and to report any malfunction therewith promptly to Landlord. Resident assumes all liability to test the detector(s) and hereby waives and exonerates Landlord from any and all liability resulting from any defective detector(s), which Resident shall not have specifically reported to Landlord.

14. **RENTER'S INSURANCE:** During the term of this Lease, and any renewal or extension thereof, Resident shall, at Resident's sole cost and expense, purchase renter's form homeowner's insurance coverage providing for personal liability (bodily injury and property damage) coverage with limits of not less than $300,000.00 each occurrence and $5,000.00 in medical payments coverage; and further, providing coverage to keep Resident's personal property on and in the Premises insured for the benefit of Resident against loss or damage resulting from broad form named perils on a replacement cost basis.

15. **LEAD, ASBESTOS, MOLD AND/OR RADON:** If Property was constructed before 1980 it may contain lead and/or asbestos containing materials. This document shall serve as constructive notice that this Property was constructed in approximately _____. Resident may have Property tested for lead, asbestos, mold and/or radon levels before occupancy. Should Resident determine that the levels of lead, asbestos, mold and/or radon are unacceptable to Resident, Resident may void this Agreement before taking possession of Property, but not later than three (3) days after entering into this Agreement with Landlord. Resident herewith acknowledges receipt of the Federal Pamphlet, Protect Your Family From Lead in Your Home, and the Lessor's disclosure form attached hereto and made a part hereof by reference.

16. **RULES AND REGULATIONS:**

RESIDENT AGREES NOT TO:

1. **PETS:** Keep any pets in or about the Property without the written permission of the Landlord.

SAMPLE LEASE

Courtesy of Aziz Abdur-Ra'oof of Keller Williams® Realty Centre

2. **SMOKING:** Smoke inside Property.

3. **APPLIANCES:** Store or install any washing machines, dryers, dishwashers, air conditioners or other appliances in the Property.

4. **FURNITURE:** Keep any water-containing furniture in the Property.

5. **WALLS AND WOODWORK:** Drive nails into the woodwork or walls of the Property, except that Resident may use standard picture hangers for hanging pictures, mirrors and the like. No adhesive hangers may be used.

6. **WALLPAPER, PAINT AND MIRRORS:** Apply contact paper, wallpaper or mirrors to the Property and will not change the type or color of paint within the Property from that used by Landlord.

7. **PORTABLE HEATERS:** Store, install or operate, in or about the Property, unvented, portable kerosene-fired heaters or propane heaters.

8. **LOCKS:** Change the locks on the doors of the Property or install additional locks, chains or other fasteners without the prior written permission of the Landlord.

9. **APPLIANCES & UTILITIES:** Misuse or overload appliances or utilities furnished by the Landlord.

10. **ADVERTISING:** Display any advertisement, sign, or notice, inside or outside the Property.

11. **WIRES AND ANTENNAS/SATELLITE DISHES:** Resident may not install any wire, cable, antenna or satellite dish for radio, television or other purposes, in or on the Property, except to the extent authorized by the Federal Communications Commission and only after compliance with Landlord's Notice of Intent to Install Antenna/Satellite Dish on Exclusive Use Area (a copy of which is available from Landlord on request).

12. **FIRE RISK:** Store in the Property or any storage area any material of any kind or description that is combustible, or would increase the risk of fire.

13. **LITTER:** Litter or obstruct the grounds.

14. **THROWING OF ARTICLES:** Throw, or allow to be thrown, anything out of the windows or doors or down the passages of the building, or from the balconies or patios.

15. **WINDOW SILLS:** Place anything on the outer edges of the sills of windows.

SAMPLE LEASE

Courtesy of Aziz Abdur-Ra'oof of Keller Williams® Realty Centre

16. **DAY CARE CENTER**: Provide, for consideration, in or about the Premises, substitute parental or guardianship care or supervision to children not related to the Resident by blood.

17. **CLOTHESLINES**: Install, erect or use exterior clotheslines.

18. **WADING POOLS**: Maintain any wading pools.

19. **ODORS**: Permit any unusual or objectionable odors to permeate or emanate from the Premises.

RESIDENT AGREES TO:

20. **CONDITION OF PREMISES**: Keep the Property in a neat, clean, good and sanitary condition.

21. **LIGHT BULBS**: Replace, at Resident's sole cost and expense, all light bulbs and tubes of the prescribed size and wattage for light fixtures and appliances within the Property.

22. **MOLD**: Remove any visible moisture accumulation in or on the Property, to thoroughly dry any such area as soon as possible after any such accumulation, and to keep the temperature and moisture in the Property at reasonable levels. In addition, Resident shall promptly notify Landlord of the presence of any water leak, excessive moisture or standing water in the Property and shall further notify Landlord of any mold growth in or on the Property and of any malfunction in any part of the heating, air conditioning or ventilation system in the Property. Resident further agrees not to block or cover any of the heating, ventilation or air conditioning ducts in the Property.

23. **PEST CONTROL**: Resident agrees to provide pest control as needed. Any infestation shall constitute a default of this Agreement.

24. **YARD CARE**: Resident will be responsible for maintaining the lawn, bushes, and trees in a neat and attractive manner. If the yard is not cared for, Landlord has the right to have it done professionally and Resident herewith agrees to pay the cost for the same.

25. **GUTTERS**: Resident shall have gutters cleaned each fall or as needed.

26. **SERVICE CHARGE**: Pay a $50.00 service charge to Landlord each time that Resident locks himself/herself out of the Premises, and requests Landlord's assistance in gaining entry to the Premises after 8:00pm on weekdays, and at any time on weekends and holidays.

SAMPLE LEASE
Courtesy of Aziz Abdur-Ra'oof of Keller Williams® Realty Centre

17. **ILLEGAL DRUGS:** If Resident, Resident's Family, employees, agents, guests and/or invitees, engage in, permit or facilitate any drug related criminal activity on or about the Premises, Resident will be deemed to have substantially and materially breached this Lease Agreement with such breach being grounds to terminate Resident's occupancy of the Premises. The term "drug-related criminal activity" means the illegal manufacture, sale, distribution, dispensing, storage, use or possession of a "controlled substance" as defined under Section 102 of the Comprehensive Drug Abuse Prevention and Control Act (21 USC 802(6), as amended) or of a "controlled dangerous substance" as defined in Article 27, Section 279 of the Annotated Code of Maryland, or to attempt, endeavor or conspire to manufacture, sell, distribute, dispense, store, use or possess a controlled dangerous substance or controlled substance.

18. **HOLDING OVER:** Should Resident hold over Property after expiration of the term of this Agreement and with the consent of Landlord, the possession shall not be construed as a renewal for the same term, but shall be construed as a month to month tenancy in accordance with the terms hereof, as applicable, and Rental Rent shall be charges at a rate 50 percent higher than the Rental Rate contained in Paragraph 3 hereinabove. There shall be no renewal of this Agreement by operation of law.

19. **LIABILITY OF LANDLORD:** Landlord shall not be liable for any injury, damage or loss to person or property caused by other tenants or other persons, or caused by theft, vandalism, fire, water, smoke, explosions or other causes unless the same is exclusively due to the omission, fault, negligence or other misconduct of the Landlord. Failure or delay in enforcing Lease covenants of other tenants shall not be deemed an omission, fault, negligence or other misconduct of the Landlord. Tenant shall defend and indemnify Landlord from any claim or liability from which Landlord is hereby exonerated.

20. **RIGHT OF ACCESS:** Landlord may enter the Property without notice toResident for inspection and maintenance during reasonable hours. Landlord shall attempt to notify Resident of the need for access, but has no obligation to do so. If locks have been changed without providing Landlord with a key, Landlord may forcibly enter without being liable for damage or unlawful entry. In case of emergency, Landlord may enter at any time. During the last sixty (60) days of occupancy, or on notification of intent to vacate, Landlord may place a sign on the Property and/or may install a lock-box and show the Property during reasonable hours. Landlord will attempt to notify Resident, but has no obligation to do so.

SAMPLE LEASE

Courtesy of Aziz Abdur-Ra'oof of Keller Williams® Realty Centre

21. DEFAULT BY RESIDENT: Should resident fail to pay any rent or other charges as and when due hereunder, or if Resident abandons the property or fails to perform any of its obligations hereunder, Landlord, at its option, may terminate all rights of Resident hereunder, unless Resident, within 24 hours after notice thereof, shall cure such default. If Resident abandons or vacates the Property, while in default of the payment of rent, Landlord may consider any property left on the Property to be abandoned and may dispose of same in any manner allowed by law, without responsibility or liability therefore. All personal property at the Property is hereby subject to a lien in favor of Landlord for payment of all sums due hereunder, to the maximum extent under law. On the adjudication of Resident in Bankruptcy, or if any facts contained in Resident's application are untrue or misleading, then, on the happening of any of said events, Resident shall be in default hereunder and Landlord may, at its option, immediately terminate this Agreement by written notice to Resident. In the event of a default by Resident, Landlord may elect to (i) continue this Agreement and enforce all of the Landlord's rights and remedies hereunder, including the right to recover the rent as it comes due, or (ii) at any time, terminate all of Resident's rights hereunder and recover from Resident all damages Landlord may incur by reason of the breach of this Agreement, including the cost of recovering the Property, and including the worth at the time of termination, or at the time of an award should a suit be instituted to enforce this provision, of the amount by which the unpaid rent for the balance of the term exceeds the amount of such rental loss which Resident proves could be reasonably avoided.

22. ABANDONMENT: Anytime the Property is left unoccupied for more than seven (7) days while rent remains unpaid without notice to Landlord, Landlord may consider the Property abandoned. Landlord may, at its option, declare this Agreement forfeited and re-rent said premises without any liability whatsoever. Resident shall be obligated to pay based on the balance of the de agreement or the early termination requirement, whichever is greater. If Resident removes or attempts to remove any personal property form the premises other than in the usual course of continuing occupancy, without having first paid monies due, Landlord shall have the right, without notice, to obtain an injunction to stop removal as Landlord has an attachment interest in the personal belongings of the non-paying Resident. Landlord shall also have the right to remove, store or dispose of any of Resident's personal property remaining on the premises after the termination of this Agreement. Any such personal property shall be considered Landlord's property, and title thereto shall vest in Landlord.

SAMPLE LEASE

Courtesy of Aziz Abdur-Ra'oof of Keller Williams® Realty Centre

23. **CROSS DEFAULT:** If Resident has entered into any other agreements concerning Property and Resident defaults on any provisions of those agreements, then the Agreement shall also be considered in default and, at the option of Landlord, this Agreement may be voided.

24. **EVICTION:** This Agreement, and all transactions contemplated hereby, shall be governed by, construed and enforced in accordance with applicable state law. Any and all claims, controversies or disputes arising out of or relating to this Agreement, or the breach thereof, which remain unresolved after direct negotiations between the Parties, then this Agreement and, without limitation to any other remedy, may take out a Dispossessory Warrant and have Resident and any other occupants and all possessions evicted and removed from Property. Should Resident answer said Dispossessory Warrant, Resident hereby agrees to pay into the registry of the trial court all monies contained on said Dispossessory Warrant plus all rents due through the court date. Landlord then has the option to continue the case in court or to notify the trial court and the Resident to have the case submitted to confidential mediation in accordance with the rules, procedures, and protocols for mediation of disputes of applicable state law then in effect. If any issues, claims or disputes remain unresolved after mediation concludes, the Parties agree to submit any such issues to binding arbitration before one/three arbitrator(s) in accordance with the rules, procedures, and protocols for arbitration of disputes of applicable state law then in effect. The parties further agree that the award of the arbitrator(s) is binding on the Parties, that all expenses of such mediation and arbitration shall be borne by the losing Party and that any judgment on the award rendered may be entered into any court of competent jurisdiction. Whenever, under the terms hereof, Landlord is entitled to possession of the Property, Resident will surrender same to Landlord in as good condition as at present, ordinary use and wear excepted, and Resident will remove all of Resident's effects therefrom, and Landlord may forthwith re-enter Property and repossess thereof and remove all persons and effects therefrom using such force as necessary without being guilty of forcible entry or detained, trespass or other tort. Resident is hereby advised that if such action is necessary, a judgment may be rendered against Resident for full damages including rent, eviction costs, and any additional costs. Resident shall also be responsible for the early termination fees as contained in paragraph 8 of this Agreement. If said costs are not paid as ordered, monies my be collected through garnishment against wages and judgments may be recorded with credit bureaus and may be assigned to a collection agency for collection with said costs of collection being the responsibility of Resident.

SAMPLE LEASE

Courtesy of Aziz Abdur-Ra'oof of Keller Williams® Realty Centre

25. **FAILURE OF LANDLORD TO ACT:** Failure of Landlord to insist on strict compliance with the terms of this Agreement shall not constitute a waiver of any violation, nor shall any acceptance of a partial payment of rent be deemed a waiver of Landlord's right to full amount.

26. **REMEDIES CUMULATIVE:** All remedies under this Agreement or by law or equity shall be cumulative. In the event that either Landlord or Resident brings legal action to enforce the terms hereof or relating to the rental Property, the prevailing party shall be entitled to all costs incurred in connection with such action including reasonable attorney's fees. In the event a collection agency becomes necessary to collect any accounts due on this Agreement, Resident agrees to pay said commission. If any term or provision of this Agreement or application thereof to any person shall be held invalid or unenforceable, the remainder of this Agreement shall not be affected thereby.

27. **NO ESTATE IN LAND:** This Agreement shall create the relationship of Landlord and Resident between Landlord and Resident; no estate shall pass out of Landlord; Resident has only a usufruct and not an estate for years.

28. **MORTGAGEE'S RIGHTS:** Resident's rights under this Agreement shall be subject to any bonafide mortgage or deed to secure debt, which is now or shall hereafter be placed on Property.

29. **LANDLORD'S PERMISSION OR CONSENT:** If any provision of this Agreement requires the written permission or consent of Landlord as a condition to any act of Resident, such written permission or consent may be granted or withheld in the sole discretion of Landlord and/or may contain such conditions as Landlord deems appropriate and shall be effective only so long as Resident complies with such conditions. Moreover, any written permission or consent given by Landlord to Resident may be modified, revoked, or withdrawn by Landlord at any time, at Landlord's sole discretion, on written notice to Resident.

30. **NOTICES:** Any notice required by this Agreement, except as otherwise set forth, shall be in writing and shall be deemed to be given if hand delivered or mailed via first class mail:

    (a) If to Resident, to the Property or the last known address of Resident;

    (b) If to Landlord, to the address as contained in Paragraph 3.

31. **ACCURACY AND RESPONSIBILITY:** Landlord has relied on the information

SAMPLE LEASE

Courtesy of Aziz Abdur-Ra'oof of Keller Williams® Realty Centre

contained in Resident's application to enter into this Agreement. Resident warrants that their rental application is true, complete and accurate. Resident

agrees that if he/she has falsified any statement in the rental application, Landlord has the right to terminate this Lease Agreement immediately and further agrees that Landlord shall be entitled to retain any fees and any prepaid rents as fair and just liquidated damages. Resident further agrees in the event Landlord exercises its option to terminate this Lease Agreement, he/she will remove him/herself, family and possessions from the Property within 24 hours of notification by Landlord.

Resident further agrees to indemnify Landlord for any damages to Property including, but not limited to, the cost of making residence suitable for renting to another Resident, and waives any right of "set-off" for the performance fee and prepaid rents which shall be forfeited as fair and just liquidated damages. It is expressly understood that this Agreement is between Landlord and each Resident, whom shall always be jointly and severally liable for the performance of every agreement and promise made herein. In the event of default by any one Resident, each remaining Resident shall be responsible for timely payment of full rent and all other provisions of this Agreement.

32. **INDEMNIFICATION:** Landlord shall not be liable for any damage or injury to Resident, or any other person, or to any property, occurring on the Property, or any part thereof, or in common areas thereof, unless such damage is the proximate result of the negligence or unlawful act of Landlord, his agents, or his employees. Resident does hereby indemnify, release, and save harmless Landlord and Landlord agents from and against any and all suits, actions, claims, judgments, and expenses arising out of or relating to any loss of life, bodily or personal injury, property damage, or other demand, claim or action of any nature arising out of or related to this Agreement or the use of this Property and premises.

33. **SEVERABILITY:** In the event that any part of this Agreement be construed as unenforceable, the remaining parts of this Agreement shall remain in full force and effect as though the unenforceable part or parts were not written into this Agreement.

34. **GENDER:** All reference to Resident herein employed shall be construed to include the plural and the singular, and the masculine shall include the feminine and neuter where the context of this Agreement may require.

SAMPLE LEASE

Courtesy of Aziz Abdur-Ra'oof of Keller Williams® Realty Centre

35. **ENTIRE AGREEMENT:** This Agreement and any attached addendum constitutes the sole and entire Agreement between the parties and no representation, promise, or inducement not included in this Agreement, oral or written, shall be binding on any party hereto. Attachments; Move-in Inspection Report; EPA Lead Paint Disclosure; EPA Lead Paint Pamphlet; Other:

IN WITNESS WHEREOF, the parties hereto have caused these presents to be signed in person or by a person duly authorized, the day and year above written. If this Agreement is not signed by all the Residents named herein and/or on rental application, the one(s) signing warrants that he or she has the authority and is acting as agent to sign for the other.

RESIDENT _____ DATE _____

RESIDENT _____ DATE _____

RESIDENT _____ DATE _____

LANDLORD _____ DATE _____

THIS DOCUMENT IS INTENDED TO BE A LEGALLY BINDING CONTRACT

If not understood, please seek the advice of an attorney before signing.

SAMPLE TENANT WALK-THROUGH LIST

A walk-through inspection of the property was completed on _____.
The following items were inspected and their condition is noted with a yes if in working order and a no if not in working order:

	Yes	No
Stove		
Wall Oven		
Refrigerator		
Ice Maker		
Dishwasher		
Built-in Microwave		
Trash Compactor		
Disposer		
Freezer		
Window Fans		
Ceiling Fans		
Attic Fans		
Smoke Detectors		
Washer		
Dryer		
Electric Air Filter		
Central Vac		
Water Softener		
Exhaust Fans		
Alarm System		
Intercom		
Garage Door Opener		
Plumbing Fixtures		
Lighting Fixtures		
Window Treatments		
Storm Windows		
Storage Shed		
Wood Stove		
Fireplace		

SAMPLE TENANT WALK-THROUGH LIST

	Yes	No
Screen Doors		
Existing Screens		
Existing Storm Doors		
Heating & AC		

Items that require repair/cleaning include:

1_____

2_____

3_____

4_____

5_____

6_____

7_____

8_____

9_____

10_____

Remarks:_____

_____

_____

_____

RESIDENT _____   DATE _____

RESIDENT _____   DATE _____

RESIDENT _____   DATE _____

LANDLORD _____   DATE _____

NOTIFICATION OF INTENT TO VACATE

Rental Address:_____

_____

Name on Lease: _____

Vacate Date:_____

Lease Expiration Date:_____

Forwarding Address:_____

_____

Lessee Signature(s):

Name_____Date_____

Name_____Date_____

As per the lease agreement, it is the lessee's responsibility to leave the premises clean and in good condition. All personal property is to be removed by the date indicated above. Any refund of security deposit funds will be sent to the forwarding address as stated above, as prescribed by law.

EXIT INTERVIEW

Please provide the following feedback so that we may ensure the highest quality service to our lessees.

Reason(s) for vacating: _____

_____

Would you say that your rental unit was:

Excellent   Good   Fair   Poor   Very Poor

Please list improvements that could be made to your unit: _____

_____

Comments: _____

_____

Date:_____

Reviewed By:_____

NOTICE OF INTENT TO ENTER DWELLING UNIT

Dear (Tenant):

This is a notification that the landlord, or a representative of the Landlord, will be entering your premises on _____ (date) _____ at (approximate time) in order to:

☐ Make the following repairs:_____

_____

☐ Show the unit to:

☐ Prospective Renters

☐ Contractors

☐ Other: _____

_____

You have the right to be present during this time. Please notify the landlord immediately if the date or time is acceptable. You are, of course, welcome to be present. If you have any questions or if the date or time is problematic, please notify the Landlord at _____ (phone number).

_____   _____

LANDLORD   DATE

AMENDMENT TO LEASE

_____ (Landlord)

and _____ (Tenant),

hereby modify and amend the lease, dated _____, regarding the

property at _____

_____ in the following details:

_____

Landlord and Tenant agree that all other terms and conditions of the Lease remain in effect throughout the term of the Lease.

Date: _____

_____

Landlord's Signature

_____

Landlord's Printed Name

RENT PAYMENT NOTICE

NOTICE OF RENT DUE

Landlord Name: _____

Landlord Address: _____

City, State, Zip: _____

Phone Number: _____

Date: _____

Tenant Name: _____

Tenant Address: _____

City, State, Zip: _____

Your rent in the amount of $_____is due on the first of every month. As of (date)_____, the rent for (address)_____ _____for the period of (month or week) has not been received.

Payment is due immediately. Bring the payment to the Landlord address listed above.

If you have already sent your payment, please call _____ (phone number) to verify that we have received it.

_____

LANDLORD SIGNATURE   DATE

_____

LANDLORD'S PRINTED NAME

HOUSING REGULATIONS
State Landlord Tenant Statutes

State	Statute
Alabama	Alabama. Code §§ 35-9-1 to -100
Alaska	Alaska Stat. §§ 34.03.010 to .380
Arizona	Arizona Rev. Stat. Ann. §§ 12-1171 to -1183; §§ 33-1301 to -1381
Arkansas	Arkansas Code Ann. §§ 18-16-101 to -306
California	California Civil Code §§ 1925-1954, 1961-1962.7, 1995.010-1997.270

HOUSING REGULATIONS
State Landlord Tenant Statutes

Colorado	Colorado. Rev. Stat. §§ 38-12-101 to -104, -301 to -302
Connecticut	Connecticut Gen. Stat. Ann. §§ 47a-1 to -51
Delaware	Delaware Code. Ann. tit. 25, §§ 5101-7013
District of Columbia	D.C. Code Ann. §§ 42-3201 to -4097, -3501.01 to -3509.03
Florida	Florida §§ 83.40-.66
Georgia	Georgia Code Ann. §§ 44-7-1 to -81
Hawaii	Hawaii Revised. Stat. §§ 521-1 to -78
Idaho	Idaho Code §§ 6-301 to -324 and §§ 55-201 to -313
Illinois	Illinois Comp. Statute. ch. 765 705/0.01-740/5
Indiana	Indiana Code Ann. §§ 32-7-1-1 to 37-7-9-10
Iowa	Iowa Code Ann. §§ 562A.1-.36
Kansas	Kansas Stat. Ann. §§ 58-2501 to -2573
Kentucky	Kentucky Rev. Stat. Ann. §§ 383.010-.715
Louisiana	Louisiana Rev. Stat. Ann. §§ 9:3201-:3259; La. Civ. Code Ann. art. 2669-2742
Maine	Maine Rev. Stat. Ann. tit. 14, §§ 6001-6046
Maryland	Maryland. Real Prop. Code Ann., §§ 8-101 to -604
Massachusetts	Massachusetts Genera. Laws Ann. ch. 186 §§ 1-21
Michigan	Michigan Comp. Laws Ann. § 554.601-.640
Minnesota	Minnesota Stat. Ann. §§ 504B.001 to 504B.471
Mississippi	Mississippi Code Ann. §§ 89-8-1 to -27
Missouri	Missouri Ann. Stat. §§ 441.005 to .880; and §§ 535.150-.300
Montana	Montana. Code Ann. §§ 70-24-101 to -25-206
Nebraska	Nebraska. Rev. Stat. §§ 76-1401 to -1449
Nevada	Nev. Rev. Stat. Ann. §§ 118A.010-.520

APPENDIX

HOUSING REGULATIONS
State Landlord Tenant Statutes

New Hampshire	New Hampshire Rev. Stat. Ann. §§ 540:1 to 540:29; 540-A:1-540-A:8
New Jersey	New Jersey State Leg. §§ 46:8-1 to – 49
New Mexico	New Mexico. Stat. Ann. §§ 47-8-1 to -51
New York	New York Real Property Law ("RPL") §§ 220-238; Real Property Actions and Proceedings Law ("RPAPL")§§ 701-853; Multiple Dwelling Law ("MDL") all; Multiple Residence Law ("MRL") all; General Obligation Law ("GOL") §§ 7-103-108
North Carolina	North Carolina. Gen. Stat. §§ 42-1 to 42-14.2; 42-25-6 to 42-76
North Dakota	North Dakota Cent. Code §§ 47-16-01 to -41
Ohio	Ohio Revised Code Ann. §§ 5321.01-.19
Oklahoma	Oklahoma Stat. Ann. tit. 41, §§ 1-136
Oregon	Oregon Revised Stat. §§ 90.100-.450
Pennsylvania	Pennsylvania. Stat. Ann. tit. 68, §§ 250.101-.510-B
Rhode Island	Rhode Island Gen. Laws §§ 34-18-1 to -57
South Carolina	South Carolina Code Ann. §§ 27-40-10 to -910
South Dakota	South Dakota Codified Laws Ann. §§ 43-32-1 to -29
Tennessee	Tennessee Code Ann. §§ 66-28-101 to -520
Texas	Texas Property Code Ann. §§ 91.001-92.354
Utah	Utah Code Ann. §§ 57-17-1 to -5, -22-1 to -6
Vermont	Vermont Statute Title 9 Chapter 137 Residential Rental Agreements
Virginia	Virginia Code Ann. §§ 55-218.1 to -248.40
Washington	Washington State. Rev. Code Ann. §§ 59.04.010-.900, .18.010-.911
West Virginia	West Virginia. Code §§ 37-6-1 to -30

HOUSING REGULATIONS
State Landlord Tenant Statutes

Wisconsin	Wisconsin Stat. Ann. §§ 704.01-.45
Wyoming	Wyoming Stat. §§ 1-21-1201 to -1211; 34-2-128 to -129

FEDERAL HOUSING REGULATIONS AND DISCLOSURE INFORMATION

Information provided by the US Department of Housing and Urban Development at
http://www.hud.gov/groups/fairhousing.cfm.

Fair Housing Act

Title VIII of the Civil Rights Act of 1968 (Fair Housing Act), as amended, prohibits discrimination in the sale, rental, and financing of dwellings, and in other housing-related transactions, based on race, color, national origin, religion, sex, familial status (including children under the age of 18 living with parents of legal custodians, pregnant women, and people securing custody of children under the age of 18), and handicap (disability). More on the Fair Housing Act:

Title VI of the Civil Rights Act of 1964

Title VI prohibits discrimination on the basis of race, color, or national origin in programs and activities receiving federal financial assistance.

Section 504 of the Rehabilitation Act of 1973

Section 504 prohibits discrimination based on disability in any program or activity receiving federal financial assistance.

Section 109 of Title I of the Housing and Community Development Act of 1974

Section 109 prohibits discrimination on the basis of race, color, national origin, sex or religion in programs and activities receiving financial assistance from HUD's Community Development and Block Grant Program.

Title II of the Americans with Disabilities Act of 1990

Title II prohibits discrimination based on disability in programs, services, and activities provided or made available by public entities. HUD enforces Title II when it relates to state and local public housing, housing assistance and housing referrals.

Architectural Barriers Act of 1968

The Architectural Barriers Act requires that buildings and facilities designed, constructed, altered, or leased with certain federal funds after September 1969 must be accessible to and useable by handicapped persons.

FEDERAL HOUSING REGULATIONS AND DISCLOSURE INFORMATION

Information provided by the US Department of Housing and Urban Development at
http://www.hud.gov/groups/fairhousing.cfm.

Age Discrimination Act of 1975

The Age Discrimination Act prohibits discrimination on the basis of age in programs or activities receiving federal financial assistance.

Title IX of the Education Amendments Act of 1972

Title IX prohibits discrimination on the basis of sex in education programs or activities that receive federal financial assistance.

Executive Order 11063

Executive Order 11063 prohibits discrimination in the sale, leasing, rental, or other disposition of properties and facilities owned or operated by the federal government or provided with federal funds.

Executive Order 11246

Executive Order 11246, as amended, bars discrimination in federal employment due to race, color, religion, sex, or national origin.

Executive Order 12892

Executive Order 12892, as amended, requires federal agencies to affirmatively further fair housing in their programs and activities, and provides that the Secretary of HUD will be responsible for coordinating the effort. The Order also establishes the President's Fair Housing Council, which will be chaired by the Secretary of HUD.

Executive Order 12898

Executive Order 12898 requires that each federal agency conduct its program, policies, and activities that substantially affect human health or the environment in a manner that does not exclude persons based on race, color, or national origin.

Executive Order 13166

Executive Order 13166 eliminates, to the extent possible, limited English proficiency as a barrier to full and meaningful participation by beneficiaries in all federally-assisted and federally conducted programs and activities.

Executive Order 13217

Executive Order 13217 requires federal agencies to evaluate their policies and programs to determine if any can be revised or modified to improve the availability of community-based living arrangements for persons with disabilities.

TIME REQUIREMENTS TO ENTER RENTAL PROPERTY BY STATE	
State	**Amount of Notice Required**
Alabama	No statute
Alaska	24 hours
Arizona	Two days
Arkansas	No statute
California	24 hours; 48 hours for initial move-out inspection
Colorado	No statute
Connecticut	Reasonable notice
Delaware	Two days
District of Columbia	No statute
Florida	12 hours
Georgia	No statute
Hawaii	Two days
Idaho	No statute
Illinois	No statute
Indiana	No statute
Iowa	24 hours
Kansas	Reasonable notice
Kentucky	Two days
Louisiana	No statute
Maine	24 hours
Maryland	No statute
Massachusetts	No notice specified
Michigan	No statute
Minnesota	Reasonable notice
Mississippi	No statute
Missouri	No statute
Montana	24 hours
Nebraska	One day
Nevada	24 hours
New Hampshire	Notice that is adequate under the circumstances

TIME REQUIREMENTS TO ENTER RENTAL PROPERTY BY STATE

New Jersey	No statute
New Mexico	24 hours
New York	No statute
North Carolina	No statute
North Dakota	Reasonable notice
Ohio	24 hours
Oklahoma	One day
Oregon	24 hours
Pennsylvania	No statute
Rhode Island	Two days
South Carolina	24 hours
South Dakota	No statute
Tennessee	No notice specified
Texas	No statute
Utah	No notice specified
Vermont	48 hours
Virginia	24 hours
Washington	Two days
West Virginia	No statute
Wisconsin	Advance notice
Wyoming	No statute

STATE STATUTE OF LIMITATIONS ON DEBTS

State	Written Contract	Oral	Promissory Notes	Open-ended or Credit Cards	State Statute: Open Accounts
AL	6	6	6	3	§6-2-37
AR	5	5	5	3	§16-56-105
AK	6	6	3	3	§09.10.053
AZ	6	3	6	3	§12-543
CA	4	2	4	4	§337

STATE STATUTE OF LIMITATIONS ON DEBTS				
State	Written Contract	Oral	Promissory Notes	Open-ended or Credit Cards	State Statute: Open Accounts
CO	6	6	6	3	§13-80-101
CT	6	3	6	3	§52-581
DE	3	3	3	4	§2-725
DC	3	3	3	3	§12-301
FL	5	4	5	4	§95.11
GA	6	4	6	4	§9-3-25
HI	6	6	6	6	HRS 657-1(4)
IA	10	5	5	5	§614.5
ID	5	4	5	4	§5-222
IL	10	5	10	5	735 ILCS 5/13-205
IN	10	6	10	6	§34-11-2
KS	6	3	5	3	§84-3-118
KY	15	5	15	5	§413.120
LA	10	10	10	3	§3-118
ME	6	6	6	6	§5-511
MD	3	3	6	3	§5-101
MA	6	6	6	6	c.260, §2
MI	6	6	6	6	§600.5807
MN	6	6	6	6	§541.05
MS	3	3	3	3	§15-1-29
MO	10	5	10	5	§516.120
MT	8	3	8	5	27-2-202
NC	3	3	5	3	§1-52(1)
ND	6	6	6	6	28-01-16
NE	5	4	5	4	§25-206
NH	3	3	6	3	382-A:3-118
NJ	6	6	6	3	25:1-5

STATE STATUTE OF LIMITATIONS ON DEBTS

State	Written Contract	Oral	Promissory Notes	Open-ended or Credit Cards	State Statute: Open Accounts
NM	6	4	6	4	§37-1-4
NV	6	4	3	4	NRS 11.190
NY	6	6	6	6	§2-213
OH	15	6	15	6	§2305.07
OK	5	3	5	3	§12-3-95
OR	6	6	6	6	§12.080
PA	4	4	4	4	§5525
RI	5	10	6	4	§6A-2-725
SC	3	3	3	3	SEC 15-3-530
SD	6	6	6	6	§15-2-13
TN	6	6	6	3	28-3-105
TX	4	4	4	4	§16.004
UT	6	4	6	4	78-12-25
VA	5	3	6	3	8.01-246
VT	6	6	5	3	§3-118
WA	6	3	6	3	RCW 4.16.080
WI	6	6	10	6	893.43
WV	10	5	6	5	§55-2-6
WY	10	8	10	8	§1-3-102

LANDLORD TOOLBOX TOOLS

- Wrenches
- Hammer
- Tape measure
- Sockets
- Screwdrivers
- Drill and bits
- Buckets
- Rags
- Paint stirrers
- Paint brushes
- Portable sander
- Extension cords
- Work light
- Tarp
- Caulk and gun
- Yardstick
- Basic hardware
- Screws
- Nuts
- Bolts
- Nails
- Work gloves
- Dust mask
- Goggles

HOME MAINTENANCE CHECKLIST

Fall – Outside

- ☐ Weather stripping
- ☐ Caulking around windows and doors
- ☐ Cracks or holes in siding
- ☐ Remove window AC units
- ☐ Take down screens
- ☐ Drain outside faucets
- ☐ Clean gutters
- ☐ Check roof for leaks
- ☐ Check flashing

HOME MAINTENANCE CHECKLIST

☐ Check chimney and flue

Fall – Inside

☐ Check Insulation

☐ Have heat pump checked

☐ Change furnace filters

☐ Check faucets for leaks

☐ Clean refrigerator coils

Spring – Outside

☐ Check all weather stripping

☐ Check caulking around windows and doors

☐ Check for cracked or peeled paint

☐ Check all screens for summer use

Spring – Inside

☐ Replace AC filters

☐ Clean dryer vent

☐ Clean stove hood

☐ Check ceiling fans

☐ Check seals on the refrigerator and freezer

☐ Clean refrigerator coils

☐ Clean fireplace

☐ Check basement for dampness

☐ Check for leaky faucets

☐ Check attic ventilation

☐ Clean blinds and drapes

LIFE EXPECTANCY OF APPLIANCES

This is the number of years you can expect an appliance to last, based on a list compiled by the National Association of Home Builders. This list will help you determine what expenses you will incur on a particular property and how soon you will incur them.

Dishwasher	10 years
Freezer	16 years
Washing Machine	13 years
Dryer	14 years
Electric Stove	17 years
Gas Stove	14 years
Central AC	15 years
Gas Water Heater	11 to 13 years
Electric Water Heater	14 years

SAMPLE AMORTIZATION TABLE

Loan of $100,000.00 borrowed on Oct. 17, 2007 at 7 Percent for 10 years

Month/Year	11/2007	12/2007	1/2008	2/2008	3/2008	4/2008
Payment ($)	1161.08	1161.08	1161.08	1161.08	1161.08	1161.08
Principal Paid ($)	577.75	581.12	584.51	587.92	591.35	594.80
Interest Paid ($)	583.33	579.96	576.57	573.16	569.73	566.28
Total Interest ($)	583.33	1163.30	1739.87	2313.03	2882.77	3449.05
Balance ($)	99,422.25	98,841.13	98,256.62	97,668.69	97,077.34	96,482.54
Month/Year	5/2008	6/2008	7/2008	8/2008	9/2008	10/2008
Payment ($)	1161.08	1161.08	1161.08	1161.08	1161.08	1161.08
Principal Paid ($)	598.27	601.76	605.27	608.80	612.35	615.92
Interest Paid ($)	562.81	559.32	555.81	552.28	548.73	545.16
Total Interest ($)	4011.87	4571.19	5127.01	5679.29	6228.02	6773.18
Balance ($)	95,884.27	95,282.51	94,677.24	94,068.44	93,456.09	92,840.17
Month/Year	11/2008	12/2008	1/2009	2/2009	3/2009	4/2009
Payment ($)	1161.08	1161.08	1161.08	1161.08	1161.08	1161.08
Principal Paid ($)	619.52	623.13	626.77	630.42	634.10	637.80
Interest Paid ($)	541.57	537.95	534.32	530.66	526.99	523.29

SAMPLE AMORTIZATION TABLE
Loan of $100,000.00 borrowed on Oct. 17, 2007 at 7 Percent for 10 years

Total Interest ($)	7314.75	7852.70	8387.02	8917.69	944.67	9967.96
Balance ($)	92,220.65	91,597.52	90,9170.75	90,340.33	89,706.23	89,068.43
Month/Year	5/2009	6/2009	7/2009	8/2009	9/2009	10/2009
Payment ($)	1161.08	1161.08	1161.08	1161.08	1161.08	1161.08
Principal Paid ($)	641.52	645.26	649.03	652.81	656.62	660.45
Interest Paid ($)	519.57	515.82	512.06	508.27	504.47	500.64
Total Interest ($)	10,487.52	11,003.35	11,515.41	12,023.68	12,528.15	13,028.78
Balance ($)	88,426.91	87,781.65	87,132.63	86,479.82	85,823.20	85,162.75
Month/Year	11/2009	12/2009	1/2010	2/2010	3/2010	4/2010
Payment ($)	1161.08	1161.08	1161.08	1161.08	1161.08	1161.08
Principal Paid ($)	664.30	668.18	672.07	676.00	679.94	683.90
Interest Paid ($)	496.78	492.91	489.01	485.09	481.15	477.18
Total Interest ($)	13,525.56	14,018.47	14,507.48	14,992.57	15,473.72	15,950.90
Balance ($)	84,498.44	83,830.27	83,158.19	82,482.20	81,802.26	81,118.35
Month/Year	5/1020	6/2010	7/2010	8/2010	9/2010	10/2010
Payment ($)	1161.08	1161.08	1161.08	1161.08	1161.08	1161.08
Principal Paid ($)	687.89	691.91	695.94	700.00	704.09	708.19
Interest Paid ($)	473.19	469.18	465.14	461.08	457.00	452.89
Total Interest ($)	16,424.09	16,893.27	17,358.41	17,819.49	18,276.49	18,729.38
Balance ($)	80,430.46	79,738.55	79,042.61	78,342.61	77,638.52	76,930.33
Month/Year	11/2010	12/2010	1/2011	2/2011	3/2011	4/2011
Payment ($)	1161.08	1161.08	1161.08	1161.08	1161.08	1161.08
Principal Paid ($)	712.32	716.48	720.66	724.86	729.09	733.34
Interest Paid ($)	448.76	444.61	440.43	436.22	431.99	427.74
Total Interest ($)	19,178.14	19,622.74	20,063.17	20,499.39	20,931.38	21,359.12
Balance ($))	76,218.00	75,501.52	74,780.86	74,056.00	72,326.91	72,593.56
Month/Year	5/2011	6/2011	7/2011	8/2011	9/2011	10/2011
Payment ($)	1161.08	1161.08	1161.08	1161.08	1161.08	1161.08
Principal Paid ($)	737.62	741.93	746.25	750.61	754.98	759.39
Interest Paid ($)	423.46	419.16	414.83	410.48	406.10	401.70
Total Interest ($)	21,782.59	22,201.75	22,616.58	23,027.06	23,433.16	23.834.85
Balance ($)	71,855.94	71,114.02	70,367.76	69,617.16	68,862.17	68,102.78
Month/Year	11/2011	12/2011	1/2012	2/2012	3/2012	4/2012
Payment ($)	1161.08	1161.08	1161.08	1161.08	1161.08	1161.08
Principal Paid ($)	763.82	768.27	772.76	777.26	781.80	786.36

SAMPLE AMORTIZATION TABLE

Loan of $100,000.00 borrowed on Oct. 17, 2007 at 7 Percent for 10 years

Interest Paid ($)	397.27	392.81	388.33	383.82	379.29	374.74
Total Interest ($)	24,232.12	24,624.93	25,013.26	25,397.08	25,776.37	26,151.09
Balance ($)	67,338.96	66,570.69	65,797.93	65,020.67	64,238.87	63,452.52
Month/Year	5/2012	6/2012	7/2012	8/2012	9/2012	10/2012
Payment ($)	1161.08	1161.08	1161.08	1161.08	1161.08	1161.08
Principal Paid ($)	790.95	795.56	800.20	804.87	809.56	814.29
Interest Paid ($)	370.14	365.53	360.89	356.22	351.52	346.80
Total Interest ($)	26,521.23	26,866.76	27,247.65	27,603.86	27,955.38	28,302.18
Balance ($)	62,661.57	61,866.01	61,065.81	60,260.94	59,451.38	58,637.10
Month/Year	11/2012	12/2012	1/2013	2/2013	3/2013	4/2013
Payment ($)	1161.08	1161.08	1161.08	1161.08	1161.08	1161.08
Principal Paid ($)	819.04	823.81	828.62	833.45	838.31	843.20
Interest Paid ($)	342.05	337.27	332.47	327.63	322.77	317.88
Total Interest ($)	28,644.23	28,981.51	29,313.97	29,641.61	29,964.38	30,282.26
Balance ($)	57,818.06	56,994.25	56,165.63	55,332.18	54,493.86	53,650.66
Month/Year	5/2013	6/2013	7/2013	8/2013	9/2013	10/2013
Payment ($)	1161.08	1161.08	1161.08	1161.08	1161.08	1161.08
Principal Paid ($)	848.12	853.07	858.05	863.05	868.09	873.15
Interest Paid ($)	312.96	308.01	303.04	298.03	293.00	287.93
Total Interest ($)	30,595.22	30,903.23	31,206.27	31,504.31	31,797.30	32,085.24
Balance ($)	52,802.54	51,949.47	51,091.42	50,228.37	49,360.28	48,487.13
Month/Year	11/2013	12/2013	1/2014	2/2014	3/2014	4/2014
Payment ($)	1161.08	1161.08	1161.08	1161.08	1161.08	1161.08
Principal Paid ($)	878.24	883.37	888.52	893.70	898.92	904.16
Interest Paid ($)	282.84	277.72	272.57	267.38	262.17	256.93
Total Interest ($)	32,368.08	32,645.80	32,918.37	33,185.75	33,447.92	33,704.84
Balance ($)	47,608.89	46,725.53	45,837.01	44,943.30	44,044.39	43,140.23
Month/Year	5/2014	6/2014	7/2014	8/2014	9/2014	10/2014
Payment ($)	1161.08	1161.08	1161.08	1161.08	1161.08	1161.08
Principal Paid ($)	909.43	914.74	920.07	925.44	930.84	936.27
Interest Paid ($)	251.65	246.35	241.01	235.64	230.24	224.81
Total Interest ($)	33,956.49	34,202.84	34,443.85	34,679.49	34,909.74	35,134.55
Balance ($)	42,230.80	41,316.06	40,395.98	39,470.54	38,539.70	37,603.43
Month/Year	11/2014	12/2014	1/2015	2/2015	3/2015	4/2015
Payment ($)	1161.08	1161.08	1161.08	1161.08	1161.08	1161.08

SAMPLE AMORTIZATION TABLE

Loan of $100,000.00 borrowed on Oct. 17, 2007 at 7 Percent for 10 years

Principal Paid ($)	941.73	947.22	952.75	958.31	963.90	969.52
Interest Paid ($)	219.35	213.86	208.33	202.78	197.19	191.56
Total Interest ($)	35,353.91	35,567.77	35,776.10	35,978.88	36,176.06	36,367.63
Balance ($)	36,661.70	35,714.48	34,761.72	33,803.42	32,839.52	31,870.00
Month/Year	5/2015	6/2015	7/2015	8/2015	9/2015	10/2015
Payment ($)	1161.08	1161.08	1161.08	1161.08	1161.08	1161.08
Principal Paid ($)	975.18	980.87	986.59	992.34	998.13	1,003.95
Interest Paid ($)	185.91	180.22	174.50	168.74	162.95	157.13
Total Interest ($)	36,553.54	36,733.76	36,908.25	37,077.00	37,239.95	37,397.08
Balance ($)	30,894.82	29,913.96	28,927.37	27,935.03	26,936.90	25,932.94
Month/Year	11/2015	12/2015	1/2016	2/2016	3/2016	4/2016
Payment ($)	1161.08	1161.08	1161.08	1161.08	1161.08	1161.08
Principal Paid ($)	1,009.81	1,015.70	1,021.62	1,027.58	1,033.58	1,039.61
Interest Paid ($)	151.28	145.38	139.46	133.50	127.51	121.48
Total Interest ($)	37,548.36	37,693.74	37,833.20	37,966.71	38,094.21	38,215.69
Balance ($)	24,923.13	23,907.44	22,885.81	21,858.23	20,824.65	19,785.04
Month/Year	5/2016	6/2016	7/2016	8/2016	9/2016	10/2016
Payment ($)	1161.08	1161.08	1161.08	1161.08	1161.08	1161.08
Principal Paid ($)	1,045.67	1,051.77	1,057.91	1,064.08	1,070.29	1,076.53
Interest Paid ($)	115.41	109.31	103/18	97.01	90.80	84.56
Total Interest ($)	38,331.10	38,440.41	38,543.59	38,640.60	38,731.40	38,815.95
Balance	18,739.37	17,687.60	16,629.69	15,565,61	14,495.33	13,418.80
Month/Year	11/2016	12/2016	1/2017	2/2017	3/2017	4/2017
Payment ($)	1161.08	1161.08	1161.08	1161.08	1161.08	1161.08
Principal Paid ($)	1,082.81	1,089.12	1,095.48	1,101.87	1,108.30	1,114.76
Interest Paid ($)	78.28	71.96	65,61	59.22	52.79	46.32
Total Interest ($)	38,894.23	38,966.19	39,031.80	39,091.01	39,143.80	39,190.13
Balance ($)	12,335.99	11,246.86	10,151.39	9,049.52	7,941.22	6,826.46
Month/Year	5/2017	6/2017	7/2017	8/2017	9/2017	10/2017
Payment ($)	1161.08	1161.08	1161.08	1161.08	1161.08	1161.08
Principal Paid ($)	1,121.26	1,127.80	1,134.38	1,1141.00	1,147.66	1,154.35
Interest Paid ($)	39.82	33.28	26.70	20.08	13.43	6.73
Total Interest ($)	39,229.95	29,263.23	39,289.93	29,310.01	39,323.44	39,330.18
Balance ($)	5,705.20	4,577.39	3,443.01	2,302.01	1,154.35	0.00

DEPRECIATION PROPERTY CLASSES TABLE Information provided by the IRS in Publication 946	
Property Class	• Personal Property (all property except real-estate)
	• Special handling devices for food and beverage manufacture
	• Special tools for the manufacture of finished plastic products, fabricated metal products, and motor vehicles
	• Property with ADR class life of 4 years or less
5-Year Property	• Information Systems; Computers/ Peripherals
	• Aircraft (of non-air-transport companies)
	• Computers
	• Petroleum drilling equipment
	• Property with ADR class life of more than 4 years and less than 10 years
7-Year Property	• All other property not assigned to another class
	• Office furniture, fixtures, and equipment
	• Property with ADR class life of more than 10 years and less than 16 years
10-Year Property	• Assets used in petroleum refining and certain food products
	• Vessels and water transportation equipment
	• Property with ADR class life of 16 years or more and less than 20 years
15-Year Property	• Telephone distribution plants
	• Municipal sewage treatment plants
	• Property with ADR class life of 20 years or more and less than 25 years
20-Year Property	• Municipal sewers
	• Property with ADR class life of 25 years or more
Property Class	• Real Property

DEPRECIATION PROPERTY CLASSES TABLE
Information provided by the IRS in Publication 946

27.5-Year Property	• Residential rental property (does not include hotels and motels)
39-Year Property	• Non-residential real property

MID-MONTH CONVENTION FOR REAL ESTATE
Information provided by Section 186 of the Internal Revenue Code

Month Asset Was Placed in Service	Years			
	1	2-9	Even Years over 10	Odd Years over 10
1	3.485%	3.636%	3.637%	3.636%
2	3.182	3.636	3.637	3.636
3	2.879	3.636	3.637	3.636
4	2.576	3.636	3.637	3.636
5	2.273	3.636	3.637	3.636
6	1.970	3.636	3.637	3.636
7	1.667	3.636	3.636	3.637
8	1.364	3.636	3.636	3.637
9	1.061	3.636	3.636	3.637
10	0.758	3.636	3.636	3.637
11	0.455	3.636	3.636	3.637
12	0.152	3.6356	3.636	3.637

BIBLIOGRAPHY

Rental Houses for the Successful Small Investor by Thomas, Suzanne.

The Complete Guide to Investing in Rental Properties by Berges, Steve.

How to Succeed and Make Money with Your First Rental House by Keipper, Douglas A. and Lyden, Sean M.

The Complete Idiot's Guide to Making Money with Rental Properties, 2nd Edition by Edwards, Brian F.

Getting Started in Rental Income by Thomsett, Michael C.

Managing Rental Properties for Maximum Profit, Revised 3rd Edition by Perry, Greg.

AUTHOR BIOGRAPHY

Teri Clark is a published author in the field of real estate, finance, and investing. Her interest in the new and different has also led to a successful online writing career. Teri has mastered the process of electronic virtual collaboration allowing her to produce nearly 100 books as an editor, researcher, freelance writer, and author. Of her five published books through Atlantic Publishing, *Private Mortgage Investing* won an Honorable Mention in Foreword Magazine's 2006 Book of the Year Award and *301 Simple Things You Can Do To Sell Your Home Now and For More Money Than You Thought* was a Finalist in the 2007 USA Best Books Awards. The North Carolina resident and her husband home school their four children. Teri contributes time weekly to service projects benefiting individuals and the community. She can be reached via her Web site: **www.teribclark. com.**

GLOSSARY

Abatement Sometimes referred to as free rent or early occupancy. A condition that could happen in addition to primary term of lease.

Absorption Rate The speed and amount of time at which rentable space, in square feet, is filled.

Accelerated Cost Recovery System A calculation for taxes to provide more depreciation for the first few years of ownership.

Accelerated Depreciation A method of depreciation where value of a property depreciates faster in the first few years after purchasing it.

Acceptance The seller's written approval of a buyer's offer.

Addendum An addition or update for an existing contract between parties.

Additional Principal Payment Additional money paid to the lender, apart from the scheduled loan payments, to pay more of the principal balance, shortening the length of the loan.

Adjustable-Rate Mortgage (ARM) A home loan with an interest rate that is adjusted periodically in order to reflect changes in a specific financial resource.

Adjusted Funds From Operations (AFFO) The rate of REIT performance or ability to pay dividends that is used by many analysts who have concerns about the quality of earnings as measured by Funds From Operations (FFO).

Adjustment Period The amount of time between adjustments for an interest rate in an ARM.

Advances The payments the servicer

makes when the borrower fails to send a payment.

Adviser A broker or investment banker who represents an owner in a transaction and is paid a retainer and/or a performance fee once a financing or sales transaction has closed.

Agency Closing A type of closing in which a lender uses a title company or other firm as an agent to finish a loan.

Agency Disclosure A requirement in most states that agents who act for both buyers or sellers must disclose who they are working for in the transaction.

Aggregation Risk The risk that is associated with warehousing mortgages during the process of pooling them for future security.

Agreement of Sale A legal document the buyer and seller must approve and sign that details the price and terms in the transaction.

Alternative Mortgage A home loan that does not match the standard terms of a fixed-rate mortgage.

Alternative or Specialty Investments
Types of property that are not considered to be conventional real estate investments, such as self-storage facilities, mobile homes, timber, agriculture, or parking lots.

Amortization The usual process of paying a loan's interest and principal via scheduled monthly payments.

Amortization Schedule Chart or table that shows the percentage of each payment that will be applied toward principal and interest over the life of the mortgage and how the loan balance decreases until it reaches zero.

Amortization Tables The mathematical tables that are used to calculate what a borrower's monthly payment will be.

Amortization Term The number of months it will take to amortize the loan.

Anchor The business or individual who is serving as the primary draw to a commercial property.

Annual Mortgagor Statement A yearly statement to borrowers which details the remaining principal balance and amounts paid throughout the year for taxes and interest.

Annual Percentage Rate (APR) The interest rate that states the actual cost of borrowing money over the course of a year.

Application Fee A fee some lenders charge that may include charges for items such as property appraisal or a credit report unless those fees are included elsewhere.

Appraisal The estimate of the value of a property on a particular date given by a professional appraiser, usually presented in a written document.

Appraisal Fee The fee charged by a professional appraiser for his estimate of the market value of a property.

Appraisal Report The written report presented by an appraiser regarding the value of a property.

Appraised Value The dollar amount a professional appraiser assigned to the value of a property in his report.

Appraiser A certified individual qualified by education, training, and experience to estimate the value of real and personal property.

Appreciation An increase in home's or property's value.

Appreciation Return The amount gained when value of real estate assets increases during current quarter.

Arbitrage The act of buying securities in one market and selling them immediately in another market in order to profit from the difference in price.

Assessment (1) The approximate value of a property. (2) A fee charged in addition to taxes in order to help pay for items such as water, sewer, street improvements, etc.

Asset A property or item of value owned by an individual or company.

Assets Under Management The amount of the current market value of real estate assets that a manager is responsible to manage and invest.

Assignee Name The individual or business to whom the lease, mortgage, or other contract has been re-assigned.

Assignment The transfer of rights and responsibilities from one party to another for paying a debt. The original party remains liable for the debt should the second party default.

Assumption The act of assuming the mortgage of the seller.

Average Common Equity The sum of the common equity for the last five quarters divided by five.

Average Downtime The number of months that are expected between a lease's expiration and the beginning of a replacement lease under the current market conditions.

Average Free Rent The number of months the rent abatement concession is expected to be granted to a tenant as part of an incentive to lease under current market conditions.

Average Occupancy The average rate of each of the previous 12 months that a property was occupied.

Average Total Assets The sum of the total assets of a company for the previous five quarters divided by five.

Back Title Letter A letter that an attorney receives from a title insurance company before examining the title for insurance purposes.

Back-End Ratio The calculation lenders use to compare a borrower's gross monthly income to their total debt.

Balance Sheet A statement that lists an individual's assets, liabilities, and net worth.

Balloon Loan A type of mortgage in which monthly payments are not large enough to repay the loan by the end of the term, and final payment is one large payment of the remaining balance.

Balloon Risk The risk that a borrower may not be able to come up with the funds for the balloon payment at maturity.

Bankruptcy A legal proceeding where a debtor can obtain relief from payment of certain obligations through restructuring their finances.

Base Loan Amount The amount that forms the basis for the loan payments.

Base Principal Balance The original loan amount once adjustments for subsequent fundings and principal payments have been made without including accrued interest or other unpaid debts.

Base Rent A certain amount that is used as a minimum rent, providing for rent increases over the term of the lease agreement.

Base Year The sum of actual taxes and operating expenses during a given year, often that in which a lease begins.

Before-Tax Income An individual's income before taxes have been deducted.

Below-Grade Any structure or part of a structure below the surface of the ground that surrounds it.

Bid The price or range an investor is willing to spend on whole loans or securities.

Bill of Sale A written legal document that transfers the ownership of personal property to another party.

Biweekly Mortgage A mortgage repayment plan that requires payments every two weeks to help repay the loan over a shorter amount of time.

Blanket Mortgage A rare type of mortgage that covers more than one of the borrower's properties.

Book Value The value of a property based on its purchase amount plus upgrades or other additions with depreciation subtracted.

Break-Even Point The point at which a landlord's income from rent matches expenses and debt.

Bridge Loan A short-term loan for individuals or companies that are still seeking more permanent financing.

Broker A person who serves as a go-between for a buyer and seller.

Build-Out Improvements to a property's space that have been implemented according to the tenant's specifications.

Build-to-Suit A way of leasing property, usually for commercial purposes, in which the developer or landlord builds to a tenant's specifications.

Capital Appreciation The change in a property's or portfolio's market value after it has been adjusted for capital improvements and partial sales.

Capital Gain The amount of excess

when the net proceeds from the sale of an asset are higher than its book value.

Capital Improvements Expenses that prolong the life of a property or add new improvements to it.

Capital Markets Public and private markets where individuals or businesses can raise or borrow capital.

Capitalization The mathematical process that investors use to derive the value of a property using the rate of return on investments.

Capitalization Rate The percentage of return as it is estimated from the net income of a property.

Carryback Financing A type of funding in which a seller agrees to hold back a note for a specified portion of the sales price.

Carrying Charges Costs incurred to the landlord when initially leasing out a property and then during the periods of vacancy.

Cash Flow The amount of income an investor receives on a rental property after operating expenses and loan payments have been deducted.

Cash-Out Refinance The act of refinancing a mortgage for an amount that is higher than the original amount for the purpose of using the leftover cash for personal use.

Certificate of Occupancy (CO) A written document issued by a local government or building agency that states that a home or other building is inhabitable after meeting all building codes.

Chapter 11 The part of the federal bankruptcy code that deals with reorganizations of businesses.

Chapter 7 The part of the federal bankruptcy code that deals with liquidations of businesses.

Class A A property rating usually assigned to those that will generate the maximum rent per square foot, due to superior quality and/or location.

Class B A good property that most potential tenants would find desirable but lacks certain attributes that would bring in the top dollar.

Class C A building that is physically acceptable but offers few amenities, thereby becoming cost-effective space for tenants who are seeking a particular image.

Clear Title A property title that is free of liens, defects, or other legal encumbrances.

Closed-End Fund A mixed fund with a planned range of investor capital and a limited life.

Closing The final act of procuring a loan and title in which documents are signed between buyer and seller and/ or their respective representation and all money concerned in the contract changes hands.

Closing Costs The expenses that are related to the sale of real estate including loan, title, and appraisal fees, and are beyond the price of the property itself.

Commercial Mortgage-Backed Securities (CMBS) A type of securities that is backed by loans on commercial real estate.

Co-Borrower Another individual who is jointly responsible for the loan and is on the title to the property.

Cost of Funds Index (COFI) An index used to determine changes in the interest rates for certain ARMs.

Co-Investment The condition that occurs when two or more pension funds or groups of funds are sharing ownership of a real estate investment.

Collateral The property for which a borrower has obtained a loan, thereby assuming the risk of losing the property if the loan is not repaid according to the terms of the loan agreement.

Collection The effort on the part of a lender, due to a borrower defaulting on a loan, which involves mailing and recording certain documents in the event that the foreclosure procedure must be implemented.

Commercial Mortgage A loan used to purchase a piece of commercial property or building.

Commercial Mortgage Broker A broker specialized in commercial mortgage applications.

Commercial Mortgage Lender A lender specialized in funding commercial mortgage loans.

Common Area Assessments Sometimes called Homeowners'

Association Fees. Charges paid to homeowners' association by individual unit owners, in a condo or planned unit development (PUD), usually used to maintain property and common areas.

Common Area Maintenance The additional charges the tenant must pay to the base rent to pay for the maintenance of common areas.

Common Areas The portions of a building, land, and amenities, owned or managed by a planned unit development (PUD) or condo's homeowners' association, used by all unit owners who share the common expense of operation and maintenance.

Community Property Property that is acquired by a married couple during the course of their marriage; considered in many states to be owned jointly, unless certain circumstances are in play.

Compound Interest Amount of interest paid on principal balance of a mortgage in addition to accrued.

Condemnation A government agency's act of taking private property, without owner's consent, for public use through the power of eminent domain.

Condominium A type of ownership in which all unit owners own the property, common areas, and buildings jointly, and have sole ownership in the unit to which they hold the title.

Contract An agreement, either verbal or written, to perform or not perform a certain thing.

Contract Rent Also known as Face Rent. The dollar amount of the rental obligation specified in a lease.

Conventional Loan A long-term loan from a non-governmental lender that a borrower obtains for the purchase of a home.

Convertible Adjustable-Rate Mortgage Mortgage that begins as a traditional ARM but contains a provision to enable borrower to change to a fixed-rate mortgage during a certain period of time.

Convertible Debt The point in a mortgage at which the lender has the option to convert to a partially or fully owned property within a certain period of time.

Convertible Preferred Stock Preferred stock that can be converted to common stock under certain conditions, specified by issuer.

Cooperative Mortgage Any loan that is related to a cooperative residential project.

Co-Signer A second individual or party who also signs promissory note or loan agreement, thereby taking responsibility for debt in the event that primary borrower cannot pay.

Cost-Approach Land Value The estimated value of the basic interest in the land, as if it were available for development to its highest and best use.

Cost-of-Sale Percentage An estimate of the expenses of selling an investment that represents brokerage commissions, closing costs, fees, and other necessary sales costs.

Coupon The token or expected interest rate the borrower is charged on a promissory note or mortgage.

Courier Fee The fee that is charged at closing for the delivery of documents between all parties concerned in a real estate transaction.

Credit An agreement in which a borrower promises to repay the lender at a later date and receives something of value in exchange.

Credit Enhancement The necessary credit support, in addition to mortgage collateral, in order to achieve the desired credit rating on mortgage-backed securities.

Credit History An individual's record which details his current and past financial obligations and performance.

Credit Life Insurance A type of insurance that pays the balance of a mortgage if the borrower dies.

Credit Rating The degree of creditworthiness a person is assigned based on his credit history and current financial status.

Credit Report A record detailing an individual's credit, employment, and residence history used to determine the individual's creditworthiness.

Credit Repository A company that records and updates credit applicants' financial and credit information from various sources.

Credit Score Sometimes called a Credit Risk Score. The number contained in a consumer's credit report that represents a statistical summary of the information.

Creditor A party to whom other parties owe money.

Current Occupancy The current percentage of units in a building or property that is leased.

Current Yield The annual rate of return on an investment, expressed as a percentage.

Debt Any amount one party owes to another party.

Debt-to-Income Ratio The percentage of a borrower's monthly payment on long-term debts divided by his gross monthly income.

Deed A legal document that conveys property ownership to the buyer.

Deed in Lieu of Foreclosure A situation in which a deed is given to a lender in order to satisfy a mortgage debt and to avoid the foreclosure process.

Deed of Trust A provision that allows a lender to foreclose on a property in the event that the borrower defaults on the loan.

Default The state that occurs when a borrow fails to fulfill a duty or take care of an obligation, such as making monthly mortgage payments.

Delinquency A state that occurs when the borrower fails to make mortgage payments on time, eventually resulting in foreclosure, if severe enough.

Delinquent Mortgage A mortgage in which the borrower is behind on payments.

Deposit Also referred to as Earnest Money. The funds that the buyer provides when offering to purchase property.

Depreciation A decline in the value of property or an asset, often used as a tax-deductible item.

Diversification The act of spreading individual investments out to insulate a portfolio against the risk of reduced yield or capital loss.

Dividend Yield The percentage of a security's market price that represents the annual dividend rate.

Dividend Distributions of cash or stock that stockholders receive.

Down Payment The variance between the purchase price and the portion that the mortgage lender financed.

Easement The right given to a non-ownership party to use a certain part of the property for specified purposes, such as servicing power lines or cable lines.

Economic Feasibility The viability of a building or project in terms of costs and revenue where the degree of viability is established by extra revenue.

Economic Rent The market rental value of a property at a particular point in time.

Effective Date The date on which the sale of securities can commence once a registration statement becomes effective.

Effective Gross Income (EGI) The total property income that rents and other sources generate after subtracting a vacancy factor estimated to be appropriate for the property.

Effective Gross Rent (EGR) The net rent that is generated after adjusting for tenant improvements and other capital costs, lease commissions, and other sales expenses.

Effective Rent The actual rental rate that the landlord achieves after deducting the concession value from the base rental rate a tenant pays.

Eminent Domain The power of the government to pay the fair market value for a property, appropriating it for public use.

Encroachment Any improvement or upgrade that illegally intrudes onto another party's property.

End Loan The result of converting to permanent financing from a construction loan.

Equity The value of a property after existing liabilities have been deducted.

Employee Retirement Income Security Act (ERISA) A legislation that controls the investment activities, mainly of corporate and union pension plans.

Errors and Omissions Insurance A type of policy that insures against the mistakes of a builder or architect.

Escrow A valuable item, money, or documents deposited with a third party for delivery upon the fulfillment of a condition.

Escrow Agreement A written agreement between an escrow agent and the contractual parties that defines the basic obligations of each party, the money (or other valuables) to be deposited in escrow, and how the escrow agent is to dispose of the money on deposit.

Escrow Closing The event in which all conditions of a real estate transaction have been met, and the property title is transferred to the buyer.

Escrow Company A neutral company that serves as a third party to ensure that all conditions of a real estate transaction are met.

Escrow Payment The funds that are withdrawn by a mortgage servicer from a borrower's escrow account to pay property taxes and insurance.

Estate The total assets, including property, of an individual after he has died.

Estimated Closing Costs An estimation of the expenses relating to the sale of real estate.

Estimated Property Taxes An estimation of the property taxes that must be paid on the property, according to state and county tax rates.

Estoppel Certificate A signed statement that certifies that certain factual statements are correct as of the date of the statement and can be relied upon by a third party, such as a prospective lender or purchaser.

Eviction The legal removal of an occupant from a piece of property.

Examination of Title A title company's inspection and report of public records and other documents for the purpose of determining the chain of ownership of a property.

Exclusive Agency Listing A written agreement between a property owner and a real estate broker in which the owner promises to pay the broker a commission if certain property is leased during the listing period.

Exclusive Listing A contract that allows a licensed real estate agent to be the only agent who can sell a property for a given time.

Fair Credit Reporting Act (FCRA) The federal legislation that governs the processes credit reporting agencies must follow.

Fair Housing Act The federal legislation that prohibits the refusal to rent or sell to anyone based on race, color, religion, sex, family status, or disability.

Fair Market Value The highest price that a buyer would be willing to pay, and the lowest a seller would be willing to accept.

Federal Housing Administration (FHA) A government agency that provides low-rate mortgages to buyers who are able to make a down payment as low as 3 percent.

Federal National Mortgage Association (FNMA) Also known as Fannie Mae. A congressionally chartered, shareholder-owned company that is the nation's largest supplier of home mortgage funds. The company buys mortgages from lenders and resells them as securities on the secondary mortgage market.

Fee Simple The highest possible interest a person can have in a piece of real estate.

Fee Simple Estate An unconditional, unlimited inheritance estate in which the owner may dispose of or use the property as desired.

Fee Simple Interest The state of owning all the rights in a real estate parcel.

FHA Loans Mortgages that the Federal Housing Administration (FHA) insures.

FHA Mortgage Insurance A type of insurance that requires a fee to be paid at closing in order to insure the loan with the Federal Housing Administration (FHA).

Finance Charge The amount of interest to be paid on a loan or credit card balance.

Firm Commitment A written agreement a lender makes to loan money for the purchase of property.

First Mortgage The main mortgage on a property.

First-Generation Space A new space that has never before been occupied by a tenant and is currently available for lease.

Fixed Costs Expenses that remain the same despite level of sales or production.

Fixed Rate An interest rate that does not change over the life of the loan.

Fixed-Rate Mortgage A loan with an unchanging interest rate over the life of a loan.

Flat Fee An amount of money that an adviser or manager receives for managing a portfolio of real estate assets.

Flex Space A building that provides a flexible configuration of office or showroom space combined with manufacturing, laboratory, warehouse, distribution, etc.

Foreclosure The legal process in which a lender takes over ownership of a property once the borrower is in default in a mortgage arrangement.

Front-End Ratio The measurement a lender uses to compare a borrower's monthly housing expense to gross monthly income.

Full-Service Rent A rental rate that includes all operating expenses and real estate taxes for the first year.

Government Loan A mortgage that is insured or guaranteed by the FHA, the Department of Veterans Affairs (VA), or the Rural Housing Service (RHS).

Grace Period A defined time period in which a borrower may make a loan payment after its due date without incurring a penalty.

Graduated Payment Mortgage A mortgage that requires low payments during the first years of the loan, but eventually requires larger monthly payments over the term of the loan that become fixed later in the term.

Grant To give or transfer an interest in a property by deed or other documented method.

Grantee The party to whom an interest in a property is given.

Grantor The party who is transferring an interest in a property.

Gross Building Area The sum of areas at all floor levels included in the principal outside faces of the exterior walls without allowing for architectural setbacks or projections.

Gross Income The total income of a household before taxes or expenses have been subtracted.

Gross Investment in Real Estate (Historic Cost) The total amount of equity and debt that is invested in a piece of real estate minus proceeds from sales or partial sales.

Gross Leasable Area The amount of floor space that is designed for tenants' occupancy exclusive use.

Gross Lease Rental arrangement in which tenant pays flat sum for rent, and landlord must pay building expenses out of that amount.

Gross Real Estate Asset Value The total market value of real estate investments under management in a fund or individual accounts, usually including total value of all equity, debt, and joint venture ownership positions.

Gross Real Estate Investment Value Market value of real estate investments held in a portfolio.

Gross Returns The investment returns generated from operating a property without adjusting for adviser or manager fees.

Ground Lease Land being leased to an individual that has absolutely no residential dwelling on the property; or if it does, the ground (or land) is the only portion of the property being leased.

Ground Rent A long-term lease in which rent is paid to the land owner, normally to build something on that land.

Growing-Equity Mortgage A fixed-rate mortgage in which payments increase over a specified amount of time with the extra funds being applied to the principal.

Guarantor The part who makes a guaranty.

Guaranty An agreement in which

265

the guarantor promises to satisfy the debt or obligations of another, if and when the debtor fails to do so.

Hard Cost The expenses attributed to constructing property improvements.

Hazard Insurance Also known as Homeowner's or Fire Insurance. Provides coverage for damage from forces such as fire and wind.

Hold-Over Tenant A tenant who retains possession of the leased premises after the lease has expired.

Home Equity Line An open-ended amount of credit based on the equity a homeowner has accumulated.

Home Equity Loan A type of loan that allows owners to borrow against the equity in their homes up to a limited amount.

Home Inspection A pre-purchase examination of the condition a home is in by a certified inspector.

Home Inspector A certified professional who determines the structural soundness and operating systems of a property.

Home Price The price that a buyer and seller agree upon, generally based on the home's appraised market value.

Homeowners' Association (HOA) A group that governs a community, condominium building, or neighborhood and enforces the covenants, conditions, and restrictions set by the developer.

Homeowners' Association Dues The monthly payments that are paid to the homeowners' association for maintenance and communal expenses.

Homeowner's Insurance A policy that includes coverage for all damages that may affect the value of a house as defined in terms of the insurance policy.

Homeowner's Warranty A type of policy homebuyers often purchase to cover repairs, such as heating or air-conditioning, should they stop working within the coverage period.

Homestead The property an owner uses as his primary residence.

Housing Expense Ratio The

percentage of gross income that is devoted to housing costs each month.

HUD (Housing and Urban Development) A federal agency that oversees a variety of housing and community development programs, including the FHA.

HUD Median Income The average income for families in a particular area, which is estimated by HUD.

HUD-1 Settlement Statement Also known as the Closing Statement or Settlement Sheet. An itemized listing of the funds paid at closing.

HUD-1 Uniform Settlement Statement A closing statement for the buyer and seller that describes all closing costs for a real estate transaction or refinancing.

HVAC Heating, ventilating, and air-conditioning.

Hybrid Debt A position in a mortgage that has equity-like features of participation in both cash flow and appreciation of property at point of sale or refinance.

Implied Cap Rate The net operating income divided by the sum of a REIT's equity market capitalization and its total outstanding debt.

Impounds The part of the monthly mortgage payment reserved in an account to pay for hazard insurance, property taxes, and private mortgage insurance.

Improvements The upgrades or changes made to a building to improve its value or usefulness.

Incentive Fee A structure in which the fee amount charged is based on the performance of the real estate assets under management.

Income Capitalization Value The figure derived for an income-producing property by converting its expected benefits into property value.

Income Property A particular property used to generate income but not occupied by the owner.

Income Return The percentage of the total return generated by the income from property, fund, or account operations.

Index Financial table that lenders use for calculating interest rates on ARMs.

Indexed Rate The sum of published index with margin added.

Indirect Costs Expenses of development other than the costs of direct material and labor that are related directly to the construction of improvements.

Individual Account Management The process of maintaining accounts that have been established for individual plan sponsors or other investors for investment in real estate, where a firm acts as an adviser in obtaining and/or managing a real estate portfolio.

Inflation Hedge An investment whose value tends to increase at a greater rate than inflation, contributing to the preservation of the purchasing power of a portfolio.

Inflation The rate at which consumer prices increase each year.

Initial Interest Rate The original interest rate on an ARM which is sometimes subject to a variety of adjustments throughout the mortgage.

Initial Public Offering (IPO) The first time a previously private company offers securities for public sale.

Initial Rate Cap The limit specified by some ARMs as the maximum amount the interest rate may increase when the initial interest rate expires.

Initial Rate Duration The date specified by most ARMs at which the initial rate expires.

Inspection Report A written report of the property's condition presented by a licensed inspection professional.

Institutional-Grade Property A variety of types of real estate properties usually owned or financed by tax-exempt institutional investors.

Insurance Binder A temporary insurance policy that is implemented while a permanent policy is drawn up or obtained.

Insurance Company Separate Account A real estate investment vehicle only offered by life insurance companies, which enables an ERISA-governed fund to avoid creating unrelated taxable income for certain types of property investments and investment structures.

Insured Mortgage A mortgage that is guaranteed by the FHA or by private mortgage insurance (PMI).

Interest Accrual Rate The rate at which a mortgage accrues interest.

Interest-Only Loan A mortgage for which the borrower pays only the interest that accrues on the loan balance each month.

Interest Paid over Life of Loan The total amount that has been paid to the lender during the time the money was borrowed.

Interest Rate The percentage that is charged for a loan.

Interest Rate Buy-Down Plans A plan in which a seller uses funds from the sale of the home to buy down the interest rate and reduce the buyer's monthly payments.

Interest Rate Cap The highest interest rate charge allowed on the monthly payment of an ARM during an adjustment period.

Interest Rate Ceiling The maximum interest rate a lender can charge for an ARM.

Interest Rate Floor The minimum possible interest rate a lender can charge for an ARM.

Interest The price that is paid for the use of capital.

Interest-Only Strip A derivative security that consists of all or part of the portion of interest in the underlying loan or security.

Interim Financing Also known as Bridge or Swing Loans. Short-term financing a seller uses to bridge the gap between the sale of one house and the purchase of another.

Internal Rate of Return (IRR) The calculation of a discounted cash flow analysis that is used to determine the potential total return of a real estate asset during a particular holding period.

Inventory The entire space of a certain proscribed market without concern for its availability or condition.

Investment Committee The governing body that is charged with overseeing corporate pension investments and developing investment policies for board approval.

Investment Manager An individual or company that assumes authority over a specified amount of real estate capital, invests that capital in assets using a separate account, and provides asset management.

Investment Policy A document that formalizes an institution's goals, objectives, and guidelines for asset management, investment advisory contracting, fees, and utilization of consultants and other outside professionals.

Investment Property A piece of real estate that generates some form of income.

Investment Strategy The methods used by a manager in structuring a portfolio and selecting the real estate assets for a fund or an account.

Investment Structures Approaches to investing that include un-leveraged acquisitions, leveraged acquisitions, traditional debt, participating debt, convertible debt, triple-net leases, and joint ventures.

Investment-Grade CMBS Commercial mortgage-backed securities that have ratings of AAA, AA, A, or BBB.

Investor Status The position an investor is in, either taxable or tax-exempt.

Joint Liability The condition in which responsibility rests with two or more people for fulfilling terms of a home loan or other financial debt.

Joint Tenancy A form of ownership in which two or more people have equal shares in a piece of property, and rights pass to the surviving owner(s) in the event of death.

Landlord's Warrant The warrant a landlord obtains to take a tenant's personal property to sell at a public sale to compel payment of the rent or other stipulation in the lease.

Late Charge Fee that is imposed by a lender when the borrower has not made a payment when it was due.

Late Payment Payment made to the lender after the due date has passed.

Lead Manager The investment banking firm that has primary responsibility for coordinating the new issuance of securities.

Lease A contract between a property owner and tenant that defines payments and conditions under which the tenant may occupy the real estate for a given period of time.

Lease Commencement Date The date at which the terms of the lease are implemented.

Lease Expiration Exposure Schedule A chart of the total square footage of all current leases that expire in each of the next five years, without taking renewal options into account.

Lease Option A financing option that provides for homebuyers to lease a home with an option to buy, with part of the rental payments being applied toward the down payment.

Leasehold Limited right to inhabit a piece of real estate held by a tenant.

Leasehold State A way of holding a property title in which the mortgagor does not actually own the property but has a long-term lease on it.

Leasehold Interest The right to hold or use property for a specific period of time at a given price without transferring ownership.

Lease-Purchase A contract that defines the closing date and solutions for the seller in the event that the buyer defaults.

Legal Blemish A negative count against a piece of property such as a zoning violation or fraudulent title claim.

Legal Description A way of describing and locating a piece of real estate that is recognized by law.

Legal Owner The party who holds the title to the property, although the title may carry no actual rights to the property other than as a lien.

Lender A bank or other financial institution that offers home loans.

Letter of Credit Promise from a bank or other party that the issuer will honor drafts or requests for payment upon complying with the requirements specified in the letter of credit.

Letter of Intent An initial agreement defining the proposed terms for the end contract.

Leverage Process of increasing the return on an investment by borrowing some of the funds at an interest rate less than the return on the project.

Liabilities Borrower's debts and financial obligations, whether long- or short-term.

Liability Insurance A type of policy that protects owners against negligence, personal injury, or property damage claims.

Lien A claim put by one party on the property of another as collateral for money owed.

Lien Waiver A waiver of a mechanic's lien rights that is sometimes required before the general contractor can receive money under the payment provisions of a construction loan and contract.

Life Cap A limit on the amount an ARM's interest rate can increase during the mortgage term.

Lifecycle The stages of development for a property: pre-development, development, leasing, operating, and rehabilitation.

Lifetime Payment Cap A limit on the amount that payments can increase or decrease over life of ARM.

Lifetime Rate Cap The highest possible interest rate that may be charged, under any circumstances, over the entire life of an ARM.

Line of Credit An amount of credit granted by a financial institution up to a specified amount.

Liquid Asset A type of asset that can be easily converted into cash.

Liquidity The ease with which an individual's or company's assets can be converted to cash without losing their value.

Loan An amount of money borrowed and repaid with interest.

Loan Officer An official representative of a lending institution who is authorized to act on behalf of the lender within specified limits.

Loan Origination The process of obtaining and arranging new loans.

Loan Origination Fee A fee lenders charge to cover costs related to arranging the loan.

Loan Servicing Process a lending institution goes through for all loans it manages. Involves processing payments, sending statements, managing the escrow/impound account, providing collection services on delinquent loans, ensuring that taxes are made, handling pay-offs and assumptions, and other services.

Loan Term Time, usually expressed in years, that a lender sets in which a buyer must pay a mortgage.

Long-Term Lease A rental agreement that will last at least three years from initial signing to the date of expiration or renewal.

Lot One of several contiguous parcels of a larger piece of land.

Maintenance Fee The charge to homeowners' association members each month for the repair and maintenance of common areas.

Maker One who issues a promissory note and commits to paying the note when it is due.

Margin A percentage that is added to the index and fixed for the mortgage term.

Market Capitalization A measurement of a company's value calculated by multiplying the current share price by the current number of shares outstanding.

Market Rental Rates The rental income a landlord could most likely ask for a property in the open market, indicated by the current rents for comparable spaces.

Market Value The price a property would sell for at a particular point in time in a competitive market.

Marketable Title Title that is free of encumbrances and can be marketed immediately to a willing purchaser.

Master Lease The primary lease that controls other subsequent leases and may cover more property than all subsequent leases combined.

Modification An adjustment in the terms of a loan agreement.

Modified Annual Percentage Rate (APR) An index of the cost of a loan based on the standard APR but adjusted for the amount of time the borrower expects to hold the loan.

Mortgage An amount of money that is borrowed to purchase a property using that property as collateral.

Mortgage Acceleration Clause A provision enabling a lender to require that the rest of the loan balance is paid in a lump sum under certain circumstances.

Mortgage Banker A financial institution that provides home loans using its own resources, often selling them to investors such as insurance companies or Fannie Mae.

Mortgage Broker An individual who matches prospective borrowers with lenders that the broker is approved to deal with.

Mortgage Insurance (MI) A policy, required by lenders on some loans, that covers the lender against certain losses that are incurred as a result of a default on a home loan.

Mortgage Interest Deduction The tax write-off the IRS allows most homeowners to deduct for annual interest payments made on real estate loans.

Mortgage Life and Disability Insurance A type of term life insurance borrowers often purchase to cover debt left when the borrower dies or becomes too disabled to make the mortgage payments.

Mortgagee The financial institution that lends money to the borrower.

Mortgagor The person who requests to borrow money to purchase a property.

Multi-Dwelling Units A set of properties that provide separate housing areas for more than one family but only require a single mortgage.

Negative Amortization An event that occurs when the deferred interest on an ARM is added, and the balance increases instead of decreases.

Net Cash Flow The total income generated by an investment property after expenses have been subtracted.

Net Investment in Real Estate Gross investment in properties minus the outstanding balance of debt.

Net Investment Income The income or loss of a portfolio or business minus all expenses, including portfolio and asset management fees, but before gains and losses on investments are considered.

Net Operating Income (NOI) The

pre-tax figure of gross revenue minus operating expenses and an allowance for expected vacancy.

Net Present Value (NPV) The sum of the total current value of incremental future cash flows plus the current value of estimated sales proceeds.

Net Purchase Price The gross purchase price minus any associated financed debt.

Net Real Estate Investment Value The total market value of all real estate minus property-level debt.

Net Returns The returns paid to investors minus fees to advisers or managers.

Net Worth The worth of an individual or company figured on the basis of a difference between all assets and liabilities.

No-Cash-Out Refinance Sometimes referred to as a Rate and Term Refinance. A refinancing transaction that is intended only to cover the balance due on the current loan and any costs associated with obtaining the new mortgage.

No-Cost Loan A loan for which there are no costs associated with the loan charged by the lender, but with a slightly higher interest rate.

No-Documentation Loan A type of loan application that requires no income or asset verification, usually granted based on strong credit with a large down payment.

Non-Compete Clause A provision in a lease agreement that specifies that the tenant's business is the only one that may operate in the property in question, thereby preventing a competitor moving in next door.

Non-Conforming Loan Any loan that is too large or does not meet certain qualifications to be purchased by Fannie Mae or Freddie Mac.

Non-Discretionary Funds The funds that are allocated to an investment manager who must have approval from the investor for each transaction.

Non-Liquid Asset A type of asset not turned into cash very easily.

Non-Performing Loan A loan agreement that cannot meet its contractual principal and interest payments.

Non-Recourse Debt A loan that limits the lender's options to collect on the value of the real estate in the event of a default by the borrower.

Notice of Default A formal written notification a borrower receives once the borrower is in default stating that legal action may be taken.

One-Year Adjustable-Rate Mortgage ARM for which the interest rate changes annually, generally based on movements of published index and specified margin.

Operating Cost Escalation A clause intended to adjust rents to account for external standards such as published indexes, negotiated wage levels, or building-related expenses.

Operating Expense The regular costs associated with operating and managing a property.

Option A condition in which the buyer pays for the right to purchase a property within a certain period of time without the obligation to buy.

Option ARM Loan A type of mortgage in which the borrower has a variety of payment options each month.

Original Principal Balance The total principal owed on a mortgage before a borrower has made a payment.

Origination Fee A fee that most lenders charge for the purpose of covering the costs associated with arranging the loan.

Originator A company that underwrites loans for commercial and/or multi-family properties.

Owner Financing A transaction in which the property seller agrees to finance all or part of the amount of the purchase.

Parking Ratio A figure, generally expressed as square footage, that compares a building's total rentable square footage to its total number of parking spaces.

Partial Payment An amount paid that is not large enough to cover the normal monthly payment on a mortgage loan.

Partial Sales The act of selling a real estate interest that is smaller than the whole property.

Partial Taking The appropriating of a portion of an owner's property under the laws of Eminent Domain.

Participating Debt Financing allowing the lender to have participatory rights to equity through increased income and/or residual value over the balance of the loan or original value at the time the loan is funded.

Payment Cap The maximum amount a monthly payment may increase on an ARM.

Payment Change Date The date on which a new payment amount takes effect on an ARM or GPM, usually in the month directly after the adjustment date.

Payout Ratio The percentage of primary earnings per share, excluding unusual items, paid to common stockholders as cash dividends during the next 12 months.

Percentage Rent The amount of rent adjusted based on percentage of gross sales or revenues the tenant receives.

Per-Diem Interest The interest that is charged or accrued daily.

Performance The changes each quarter in fund or account values that can be explained by investment income, realized or unrealized appreciation, and the total return to the investors before and after investment management fees.

Performance-Based Fees The fees that advisers or managers receive that are based on returns to investors.

Periodic Payment Cap The highest amount that payments can increase or decrease during a given adjustment period on an ARM.

Periodic Rate Cap The maximum amount that the interest rate can increase or decrease during a given adjustment period on an ARM.

Permanent Loan A long-term property mortgage.

Personal Property Item belonging to a person that is not real estate.

Pre-Approval The complete analysis a lender makes regarding a potential borrower's ability to pay for a home as well as a confirmation of the proposed amount to be borrowed.

Pre-Approval Letter The letter a

lender presents that states the amount of money they are willing to lend a potential buyer.

Preferred Shares Certain stocks with a prior distributions claim up to a defined amount before common shareholders may receive anything.

Pre-Leased A certain amount of space in a proposed building that must be leased before construction may begin or a certificate of occupancy may be issued.

Prepaid Interest The amount of interest paid before its due date.

Prepayment The money paid to reduce principal balance of a loan before the date it is due.

Prepayment Penalty A penalty charged to the borrower when he pays off a loan before the planned maturity date.

Prepayment Rights The right a borrower is given to pay the total principal balance before the maturity date free of penalty.

Prequalification The initial assessment by a lender of a potential borrower's ability to pay for a home

as well as an estimate of how much the lender is willing to supply to the buyer.

Price-to-Earnings Ratio The comparison that is derived by dividing the current share price by the sum of the primary earnings per share from continuing operations over the past year.

Primary Issuance The preliminary financing of an issuer.

Prime Rate The best interest rate reserved for a bank's preferred customers.

Prime Tenant The largest or highest-earning tenant in a building or shopping center.

Principal The amount of money originally borrowed in a mortgage, before interest is included and with any payments subtracted.

Principal Balance The total current balance of mortgage principal not including interest.

Principal Paid over Life of Loan The final total of scheduled payments to the principal that the lender calculates to equal the face amount of the loan.

Principal Payments The lender's return of invested capital.

Private Debt Mortgages or other liabilities for which an individual is responsible.

Private Equity A real estate investment that has been acquired by a noncommercial entity.

Pro Rata The proportionate amount of expenses per tenant for the property's maintenance and operation.

Property Tax The tax that must be paid on private property.

Public Debt Mortgages or other liabilities for which a commercial entity is responsible.

Public Equity A real estate investment that has been acquired by REITs and other publicly traded real estate operating companies.

Purchase Agreement Written contract buyer and seller sign defining the terms and conditions under which a property is sold.

Qualified Plan Any employee benefit plan that the IRS has approved as a tax-exempt plan.

Qualifying Ratio The measurement a lender uses to determine how much they are willing to lend to a potential buyer.

Rate Cap The highest interest rate allowed on a monthly payment during an adjustment period of an ARM.

Rate Lock The commitment of a lender to a borrower that guarantees a certain interest rate for a specific amount of time.

Real Property Land and anything else of a permanent nature that is affixed to the land.

Real Rate of Return The yield given to investors minus an inflationary factor.

Realtor A real estate agent or broker affiliated with the National Association of Realtors.

Recourse Option a lender has for recovering losses against the personal assets of a secondary party who is also liable for a debt in default.

Refinance Transaction The act of paying off an existing loan using the funding gained from a new loan that uses the same property as security.

Rehab Short for Rehabilitation. Refers to an extensive renovation intended to extend the life of a building or project.

Real Estate Investment Trust (REIT) A trust corporation that combines the capital of several investors for the purpose of acquiring or providing funding for real estate.

Remaining Balance The amount of principal on a home loan that has not yet been paid.

Remaining Term The original term of the loan after the number of payments made has been subtracted.

Renewal Option A clause in a lease agreement that allows a tenant to extend the term of a lease.

Renewal Probability The average percentage of a building's tenants expected to renew terms at market rental rates upon the lease expiration.

Rent Commencement Date Date at which a tenant begins paying rent.

Rent Loss Insurance A policy that covers loss of rent or rental value for a landlord due to any condition that renders the leased premises inhabitable, thereby excusing the tenant from paying rent.

Rent The fee paid for the occupancy and/or use of any rental property or equipment.

Rentable/Usable Ratio A total rentable area in a building divided by the area available for use.

Rental Growth Rate The projected trend of market rental rates over a particular period of analysis.

Rent-Up Period The period of time following completion of a new building when tenants are actively being sought and the project is stabilizing.

Repayment Plan An agreement made to repay late installments or advances.

Replacement Cost Projected cost by current standards of constructing a building equivalent to the building being appraised.

Rescission The legal withdrawing of a contract or consent from the parties involved.

Retail Investor An investor who sells interests directly to consumers.

Return on Assets The measurement of the ability to produce net profits efficiently by making use of assets.

Return on Equity The measurement of the return on the investment in a business or property.

Return on Investments The percentage of money gained as a result of certain investments.

Right of Ingress or Egress Option to enter or leave premises in question.

Risk Management A logical approach to analyzing and defining insurable and non-insurable risks while evaluating the availability and costs of purchasing third-party insurance.

Road Show A tour of the executives of a company that is planning to go public, during which the executives travel to a variety of cities to make presentations to underwriters and analysts regarding their company and IPO.

Sales Contract An agreement both buyer and seller sign defining the terms of a property sale.

Second Mortgage A secondary loan obtained on a piece of property.

Secured Loan A loan secured by some sort of collateral.

Securitization Converting a non-liquid asset into a tradable form.

Security Deposit An amount of money a tenant gives to a landlord to secure the performance of terms in a lease agreement.

Seller Financing A type of funding in which the borrower may use part of the equity in the property to finance the purchase.

Servicing Collecting mortgage payments from borrowers as well as related responsibilities.

Space Plan A chart or map of space requirements for a tenant.

Stabilized Occupancy The best projected range of long-term occupancy that a piece of rental property will achieve after existing in the open market for a reasonable period of time with terms and conditions that are comparable to similar offerings.

Step-Up Lease (Graded Lease) A lease agreement that specifies certain increases in rent at certain intervals during the complete term of the lease.

Subordinate Loan A second or third mortgage obtained with the same property being used as collateral.

Subordinated Classes Classes that have the lowest priority of receiving payments from underlying mortgage loans.

Subsequent Rate Adjustments The interest rate for ARMs that adjusts at regular intervals, sometimes differing from the duration period of the initial interest rate.

Subsequent Rate Cap Maximum amount the interest rate may increase at each regularly scheduled interest rate adjustment date on an ARM.

Surface Rights A right or easement usually granted with mineral rights that enables the holder to drill through the surface.

Survey A document or analysis containing the precise measurements of a piece of property as performed by a licensed surveyor.

Taking Similar to condemning, or any other interference with rights to private property, but physical seizure or appropriation is not required.

Tenancy by the Entirety A form of ownership held by spouses in which they both hold title to the entire property with right of survivorship.

Tenancy in Common A type of ownership held by two or more owners in an undivided interest in the property with no right of survivorship.

Tenant (Lessee) A party who rents a piece of real estate from another by way of a lease agreement.

Tenant at Will A person who possesses a piece of real estate with the owner's permission.

Tenant Improvement (TI) Allowance The specified amount of money that the landlord contributes toward tenant improvements.

Tenant Improvement (TI) The upgrades or repairs made to the leased premises by or for a tenant.

Tenant Mix The quality of the income stream for a property.

Term The length that a loan lasts or is expected to last before it is repaid.

Total Acres Total land area contained in a real estate investment.

Total Expense Ratio The comparison of monthly debt obligations to gross monthly income.

Total Loan Amount The basic amount of the loan plus any additional financed closing costs.

Total Monthly Housing Costs The amount that must be paid each month to cover principal, interest, property taxes, PMI, and/or either hazard insurance or homeowners' association dues.

Total of All Payments The total cost of the loan after figuring the sum of all monthly interest payments.

Total Principal Balance The sum of all debt, including the original loan amount adjusted for subsequent payments and any unpaid items that may be included in the principal balance by the mortgage note or by law.

Total Return The final amount of income and appreciation returns per quarter.

Townhouse An attached home not considered to be a condominium.

Truth-in-Lending The federal legislation requiring lenders to fully disclose the terms and conditions of a mortgage in writing.

Two-Step Mortgage An ARM with two different interest rates: one for the loan's first five or seven years and another for the remainder of the loan term.

Underwriting The process during which lenders analyze the risks a particular borrower presents and set appropriate conditions for the loan.

Underwriting Fee A fee that mortgage lenders charge for verifying information on the loan application and making a final decision on approving the loan.

Usable Square Footage The total area included within the exterior walls of the tenant's space.

Vacancy Factor The percentage of gross revenue that pro-forma income statements expect to be lost due to vacancies.

Vacancy Rate The percentage of space that is available to rent.

Vacant Space Existing rental space that is presently being marketed for lease minus space that is available for sublease.

Value-Added A phrase advisers and managers generally use to describe investments in underperforming and/or under-managed assets.

Variable Rate Mortgage (VRM) A loan in which the interest rate changes according to fluctuations in particular indexes.

Variable Rate Also called adjustable rate. The interest rate on a loan that varies over the term of the loan according to a predetermined index.

Verification of Employment (VOE) The confirmation statement a borrower's employer may be asked to sign in order to verify the borrower's position and salary.

Waiting Period The period of time between initially filing a registration statement and the date it becomes effective.

Weighted-Average Rental Rates The average ratio of unequal rental rates across two or more buildings in a market.

Zoning The act of dividing a city or town into particular areas and applying laws and regulations regarding the architectural design, structure, and intended uses of buildings within those areas.

INDEX

T